INTERIOR BLISS

INTERIOR BLISS

HOW TO DESIGN LIKE A PRO WITHOUT BREAKING THE BANK

JONATHAN HOPP

For information on distribution rights, royalties, derivative works or licensing opportunities on behalf of this content or work, please contact the publisher at the address below or via email info@nolimitpublishinggroup.com.

COMPANIES, ORGANIZATIONS, INSTITUTIONS, AND INDUSTRY PUBLICATIONS: Quantity discounts are available on bulk purchases of this book for reselling, educational purposes, subscription incentives, gifts, sponsorship, or fundraising. Special books or book excerpts can also be created to fit specific needs such as private labeling with your logo on the cover and a message from a VIP printed inside.

No Limit Publishing Group
123 E Baseline Road, D-108
Tempe AZ 85283
info@nolimitpublishinggroup.com

This book was printed in the United States of America

No Limit Publishing
No Limit Enterprises, LLC
1601 E 69th Street, Suite 200
Sioux Falls, SD 57108

TESTIMONIALS

"I was astonished by Jonathan's finish selection. He put together materials I had never seen, and they were absolutely perfect for my home. My friends couldn't believe the transformation that had taken place; it didn't even look like the same house. I couldn't be more pleased with Jonathan's work."

–Michelle Poletti

"My husband and I were overwhelmed with the task of remodeling our home until Jonathan stepped in. He knew exactly what to do and handled the project with grace and ease. We once thought of this home as temporary, but since Jonathan redesigned it, we never want to move."

–Helen Palmer

"Jonathan's design talents never cease to amaze me. He has an amazing ability to just *see* the potential in every space that he designs (or redesigns). Give him an assortment of decorative objects and not only will he arrange them in ways that I, as the client, have never imagined, he will do it so quickly you would have thought someone waved a magic wand! He really loves what he does and is an absolute pleasure to work with. I would never do a project without him."

–Diana Robinson

"Jonathan knows how to imprint character into every room that he designs. Each one of my home's bathrooms has a unique look that ties in seamlessly with the rest of the house. Because of Jonathan, I can now say that I live in the home of my dreams."

–Michelle Hogan

"Downsizing from a five bedroom house to a two bedroom condo seemed challenging until Jonathan worked his magic. He was able to use what we had to create an inviting and comforting interior. I never thought I'd live in such a beautiful home."

–Edie Goldberger

"Thank you for sending the first chapter. Jonathan, I don't like a lot of things like that and quite frankly don't find books like that very helpful. I've paged through *many* in the last months. *However, I loved yours*. It totally spoke to me and my situation. I found it fantastically practical—I've never seen that approach in any of the books I've picked up. I've started putting together my file! I'm so happy—I have collected some great pictures and add weekly to my style file! I can see my room coming together. Thank you so much!"

–Mimi and Bob

CONTENTS

OPENING

ENLIGHTENED CHOICE

While creating a look to tell the story of a particular room or home, it is important to illustrate not only what *is* fashionable, but what *will be* fashionable for a long time to come. Most people don't have an unlimited budget, and even those who are able to add a few more zeros to their spending limit can appreciate getting the look they love at a great price. We have all felt the excitement of finding "just the right thing" at such a sale price it seems as if we were being paid to own it. The idea, when designing a room, is to find pieces that are the perfect choice, while doing it inexpensively. To make that happen requires education or a game plan. As an interior designer, I frequently make decisions more complicated than most. Is the item the right scale? Does it coordinate with the pieces selected? Can it be used with different pieces to create a number of looks? Interior design considers fashion, flexibility, durability, and price when committing to furniture, art, accessories, and lighting. Designing a room creates a sense of bliss when everything comes together, and every piece contributes to the overall harmony. Bliss is the feeling of delight we have as we enjoy our homes and have a place that we love.

What has happened to the economy during the past several years requires making a budget (and sticking to it) more important than ever. Each of us, including me, has felt the pinch. It seems we no longer have the freedom to design with unlimited funds, yet we still want to come home to a place that is welcoming, makes us feel comfortable and even proud. Our new challenge is to discover how to create the perfect look without compromise and breaking the bank. Budgets are a guide keeping us on track. In creating a list of things we want, we build a portfolio of ideas that guides us in knowing what to buy, when to buy it, and what's the best design for our financial plan.

Whether it's a watch, a pair of shoes, or a lamp, we all get a rush of joy when we know we have gotten a good deal. A good designer knows where to find those bargains, while knowing when it's appropriate to go beyond our budget to make the best selection. In design school, I was told that interior design is enlightened choice. As we gather more knowledge, we proceed with confidence in making our decisions. Bliss is the certainty that the more you know, the more certain your success is.

I like nothing better than to tell people how much I have spent on something when I know I have gotten a great deal. It's like a small victory and something to be proud of, although not everything will be that way. There are times when it is reasonable to pay more for particular items. When working with my clients, I teach them when they need to fork over the bigger bucks, knowing the money is well spent. We have done our research and have considered the item's function, design, sturdiness, and value. We know that this item is necessary for the room. It also means that we understand that other things will have to wait while the budget catches up. We don't feel bad spending a little more for the perfect sofa because we are aware that we will have to be more budget-conscious when buying the room's other items.

A sunburst mirror provides a dramatic back drop for a simple arrangement in an entry hall.

In a large living room, an arrangement of four large English arm lounge chairs provides important scale in the space while creating an intimate area for gathering.

A tool that I find invaluable is a selection of pictures that illustrate a client's likes and dislikes. This "design file" becomes our point of reference in making decisions about everything from cabinet knobs to paint colors, flea market or modern. Start pulling pictures of things you like—pictures of anything from siding on a house to ways to display collections. This file becomes the reference point from which decisions are drawn. When designing a project, I refer to the file frequently to keep myself on track. When I am working on a project, I gather all the pictures that remind me of the style and create a binder for the project. When a decision needs to be made, out comes the file. It's the first place I look when pondering a particular problem.

An advantage of a design file is that it helps get rid of all the magazines lying around. After having moved a multitude of magazines through the years, I became aware that all I did was that—move them. They were never referenced because it would take a long time to find the specific magazine and then the specific article. After one afternoon of editing, 200 magazines made it into recycling, and the items I wanted were easily accessible. While making the file and looking for pictures, you will find things that naturally attract you. These represent your style, and often you will find you become attracted to similar things. The file narrows down all the options to a few that are easily accessed.

The modern mix of classic furniture and ethnic accessories create a timeless dining room.

The fastest way to get into trouble when designing a home is not knowing what you want. Aside from the wealth of choices that make our heads spin, we may be unaware of the solution right in front of our faces. This lack of knowledge slows down the project and usually means it will end up over budget. The best way to avoid this is by doing your homework. The more we know, the better are the choices that we make.

Accessorize rooms with pieces you love. Good design lasts a lifetime.

It can be as simple as looking around. The best place to begin is magazines. Start by tearing out pictures of things you like and begin creating a design file of colors, shapes, periods, and designs that catch your attention. Draw inspiration from your own existing lifestyle and the architecture of your home to draw you to ideas in the pictures you find. Even if the items are outside your budget now, often there is a way to get the look you want. Once you know an item will work in your design, start researching by visiting websites. When I go online to my favorite sites, I always check the "sale" and "clearance" sections first. Many times I find the perfect thing at a fraction of the original price.

There are a multitude of publications that focus on home design and décor. In recent years, it seems that many have gone out of business. The good ones are still around offering design tips, new product information, and ideas for saving money. Although your particular style might not be reflected by the target audience for the magazine, do not overlook the individual pieces and ideas these magazines have to offer.

One of my favorite design magazines is *Country Living*. I like an urban country look, which is vintage simplified and mixed with more modern elements. Even if your look does not venture into this style, the magazine is good for ideas and designs that are pretty straight-forward. I think I have always had a subscription to *House Beautiful*. Every issue features a different style, which keeps the magazine fresh.

There is a section on color that I think is helpful, and it highlights *best products* sifting through the wealth of new merchandise to show the best and smartest in different categories. There is always something I would not otherwise see. If your style is more eclectic, *Elle Decor* is for you. This magazine often features up-and-comers in the design industry that reflect an innovative approach to design. One of my favorite sections in *Elle Decor* is the "10 Best…" This section features the best dressers, sofas, chairs, and so forth. While the pieces in the magazine might be out of my price range, it is a great reference for learning different styles. For inspiration, *Veranda* magazine is one of the best. The pictures are fantastic, and the designs are gorgeous. Finally, *Renovation Style* is a wonderful resource for styles, using color, and learning about design. It also highlights products from a multitude of manufacturers; that information can get you started doing some online research.

Another way to build your design file is as simple as shopping. It is easy to be inspired by others' designs, and when you are, don't hesitate to add those ideas to your portfolio. Flea markets, consignment shops, retail stores, and antique shops almost always have something that will work. Recognize that the lamp you found may be the perfect choice with the addition of a new lampshade, or the bench will work as a table in front of a sofa. The goal is to start discovering what you really want, and the only way to do that is by doing your homework.

I get inspiration everywhere I go. I never get bored in waiting rooms or airports because I look at the furniture or environment and wonder about the inspiration of the designer. Hiking along the lake, I think about using bark or moss, and I look at the windows on houses and the colors I see around me. I do the same thing in high-end retail stores, exclusive boutiques, and antique shops. In the context of design, they all serve the purpose— enlightenment. The key is to shop everywhere but purchase discriminately.

Hopp Tips:

- Start a design file by tearing out pictures from magazines. Toss the rest of the magazine into the recycling bin. It saves on clutter and recycling feels great!

- Visit an antique store or flea market. Buy a gently used treasure for your home collection.

- Go to a new hotel or trendy restaurant and get inspired by their interiors.

- Go shopping with your camera or cell phone. Take pictures of items for inspiration. This can be furniture, fabrics, lamps, plants or paint colors. Use these pictures as part of your design file.

- Surf the internet with keywords "budget interiors" "decorating resources" "cheap chic." You'll be busy for hours and find amazing resources.

Sites for inspiration, shopping and reading:

- Traditionalhome.com
- Housebeautiful.com
- Countryliving.com
- Elledecor.com
- Veranda.com
- Potterybarn.com
- Target.com

High-end stores and hotels are good places to look for ideas. Both have the latest in design trends. Hotels are interesting because the designers are working on a theme, such as modern, traditional, hip. The selections must be durable to stand up to the rigors of constant use, and they must hide stains and clean easily. If you have looked at one of the more recent hotel designs like the W Hotels and smaller boutique inns such as Joie De Vivre hotels in California, you will see what I am talking about. Retail shops are a wealth of ideas. I am not always buying; I am looking—for inspiration. Even if I am not interested in buying, I enjoy looking at the prices and then finding where I can purchase the same look without the huge price attached. The point is to get ideas that will work in your own design plan. Use your cell phone to take pictures and add something to your design file. It will come in handy when shopping somewhere else. (Make sure to take a picture of price tags on items that have them. That way, it is easy to figure out where you saw it.)

I often comb vintage shops to find interior treasures that may be the perfect piece for a design concept. Treasures may be as simple as a woven hamper, antique ceramics, or an unusual lamp. Vintage shops are excellent sources for finding unique accessories (or to start building a collection). Often it is the little stuff that brings a room together.

Box stores like Target are another favorite. You can find inexpensive art, mirrors, lamps, and bedding that will keep you on budget. Target, in particular, commissions celebrity designers to create product lines that reflect the designer's look. The advantage is you can get the essence of a designer without spending what you might expect if you were to purchase from one of that person's boutiques. Pottery Barn and Restoration Hardware are other retail favorites because they change inventory with the seasons. When they change inventory, that means stuff goes on sale! These stores also have extensive online catalogs. Items not available in stores are often online—and remember that items bought online can always be returned.

Whatever your approach to getting started, your design file will save you a lot of work. Something as simple as a picture to show a contractor, store clerk, or interior designer is the best way to communicate an idea. Write on the picture what you like, so you don't forget. As you sift through the huge number of ideas that you have accumulated from doing your homework, you are getting an education in interior design. Enlightened choice brings you to a new level of design that will allow you to proceed with confidence as you create the dream that you envision.

Gorgeous red and gold pillows enliven a neutral color scheme that's repeated in the striped chairs. While this room is symmetrical, the use of different styled chairs along with oversized chests as end tables provides a more interesting compostion than using matching pieces. Crystal lamps, candlesticks, decorative boxes and framed architectural drawings provide finishing touches.

PART ONE
DESIGN BASICS

CHAPTER 1
FAUX REAL?

REAL PLANTS VERSUS ARTIFICIAL PLANTS

"My fake plants died because I did not pretend to water them."
–Mitch Hedberg

Flowers have long been a source of beauty and stimulation for mankind. From Monet's water lilies to Van Gogh's sunflowers, from William Shakespeare to Walt Whitman, flowers have inspired many of the world's greatest creative minds. Often representing some of our fondest feelings, such as love, peace, calm, and happiness, flowers are a wonderful additional to any home. Bringing the outdoors in with a bit of green has the magical ability to bring a room to life.

To me, plants fall into an accessory category. Have you ever noticed that it is the little things that make rooms feel more inviting? I have never been one of those that thought "less is more." Sometimes it is still less. The best rooms I have been in included plants, books, mementos, art, and color. This chapter addresses *permanent botanicals*. This can be anything from a dried floral wreath to silk arrangements. A simple arrangement in a room with no natural light can do wonders.

Every designer has his or her own opinion on whether or not using artificial plants is acceptable. My opinion is if someone doesn't want to worry about caring for plants, and they will end up dead or scrawny anyhow, then artificial plants are perfectly acceptable! Why should anyone be denied the joy and beauty of having plants indoors? Done well, artificial are beautiful and more available than ever.

With such an enormous assortment of silk flowers and artificial plants available today, it can be daunting to discern which varieties will look best in your home. Many companies have greatly improved the quality of their artificial plants, making it possible to purchase fantastic materials at a great price. Pier 1 and Restoration Hardware are two places that I frequently recommend for finding decorative plants and flowers. Also, more and more companies are creating fresh new looks that can really up the wow factor of your plant or floral arrangement. Search for items that you would love to have in your home but would not be able to maintain or grow if you were working with live plants. Black bamboo is an out-of-the-ordinary plant that is probably not reasonable for people to purchase live; however, it works very well as an artificial plant in the home when placed in the right container.

Get creative when potting plants. This vintage suitcase is a clever container for hydrangeas and creates a memorable dining table experience.

When designing a floral arrangement, don't skimp on the flowers. The fuller the better!

Dining rooms are one of my favorite rooms to enhance with artificial plants. If you are someone who enjoys the fresh look of flowers in your formal dining room, consider using artificial stems. Because real cut flowers have to be replaced frequently, they aren't cost-effective for most of us. The flowers end up looking tired and droopy after a short period of time and need to be replaced on a weekly basis. So while fresh flowers are a beautiful touch to your home, they may not be the most practical solution. A good artificial arrangement is as effective as real flowers, and with the removal or addition of a few different flowers or branches, the arrangement can be easily changed for a more seasonal look.

There are a few rules to follow when you are selecting "permanent" plants:

- Choose foliage and flowers that look realistic. Go with your gut instinct; if it looks fake when you first see it, don't buy it.

- Don't use plants that are not native to the area in which you live. A cactus will look strange and out of place in most Northern climates.

- Avoid premade arrangements. There is such a thing as too perfect, and it's a dead giveaway that says "fake plant." Shake up your creativity and choose florals and foliage that speak to you.

Hopp Tips:

- Find an interesting tree branch and use it as a centerpiece, or part of a grouping with other found objects. I am always picking up seed pods, pinecones and shells.

- Buy a tree; place it in an attractive container for a neglected corner in a room. Greenery makes rooms come alive. If you don't have a green thumb, buy an artificial plant. I've found great fake black bamboo plants the size of trees online.

- Use a vase or container in multiples for a fresh clever decoration. A collection of mismatched bud vases with a single stem in each is charming and inexpensive. A series of pots with flowering plants lined up on a mantle is a perfect way to freshen a room.

- Decorate your existing hurricane with shells, sand, pine cones or flowers floating on water. Artificial flowers are a great option as well. It's a dramatic look and doesn't take any time to complete.

- Be generous when you use artificial flowers. Abundant arrangements are more striking to look at.

Artificial succulents create a dramatic arrangement around candles. Easily arranged, they can be replaced seasonally with pine cones, shells or other greenery.

Sites with great artificial greenery, trees and plants:

- Silkflowers.com – trees to single stems
- Belacor.com – wreaths, arrangements
- Pier1.com - single stems, succulents, trees and wreaths
- Potterybarn.com – great seasonal flowers
- Restorationhardware.com – topiaries, zinc pots
- Overstock.com – trees, large grasses and exotic plants

If you are someone who really does prefer to have live plants, find ones that are easy to grow and maintain, or be willing and able to change them frequently. You need to give yourself permission to throw away old plants. Think of greenery as an accessory rather than a pet or a project. For example, terra-cotta pots with bright flowers in them are a great family room accessory, but when the plants begin to die, toss them out. It really is okay! And while we're on the subject of terra-cotta, don't use the green plastic pot real plants often come in as your display container. The pot or urn in which you place your plant—live or artificial—is often as much a part of the décor as the plant itself. Be adventurous in the containers you use, and consider the overall look of the room the plant will go in before making a decision. There are so many more options than a traditional glass vase; go for a zinc pot, an old pitcher, a vintage basket, or a colorful ceramic vase instead. I love repurposing found items as part of my floral displays. An antique suitcase filled with hydrangeas was the perfect centerpiece for a dining room in a shabby chic home I staged, and guests of my home were always tickled by the vintage urinal I used to hold fresh mums.

Whether you choose to use real greenery or artificial plants, look online and at magazines for inspiration. There are so many ideas out there that one is bound to inspire you. Be smart, know what you want, and do your research before spending any money. The goal in using greenery and flowers is to make the entire room look as beautiful and complete as possible, and it's those last little touches that are often the most important.

Choose flowers that look realistic, and be creative when selecting containers for display

CHAPTER 2
ROSE TINT MY WORLD

CHOOSING YOUR COLOR PALETTE

"I owe my color sense to crayons."
–Angelo Rafael Donghia, *New York Times*

Color plays an important role in human expression. It has the power to affect our mood and influence our outlook, even when we're not aware of it. Red stimulates the appetite, orange evokes excitement, and blue promotes relaxation. Because color is such a powerful element in design, it's important to plan your color palette wisely.

Most people are very intimidated by the task of selecting a color scheme. All too often I see clients play it safe with neutrals instead of going for the colors that they truly love. The end result is often a real snoozer of a room: lifeless, bland, and completely lacking personality. Luckily, I have developed some helpful tips for leaving behind the boring world of beige and embracing the joyful bounty of colors.

To avoid getting lost in a sea of paint samples and color swatches, I suggest starting with the information you already have on hand: your wardrobe! What colors come up over and over in your clothing selection? Do you prefer cool blues and greens or invigorating yellows and reds? This is often a good indication of what colors you would like to be surrounded by in your home. What colors do you find yourself drawn to in art, flowers, and even jewelry? And finally, can you live with those colors and feel comfortable with them in your place to unwind and gather with family and friends? In short, what colors bring you bliss?

Here's some good news that should help alleviate some of the stress of creating a color scheme: You don't have to have boldly colored walls for your family room to be colorful. Instead, I recommend picking a classic, neutral hue for the walls and adding splashes of color in your furniture, fabric, and art. Not only will it make it easy to coordinate the pieces you introduce into the space, but it will also give you lots of wiggle room for when you're ready to update pieces or change your look altogether.

I love white. It's one of my favorite colors to use in a home, and it comes in so many different shades and variations that it works in literally any situation. Despite my love of white, it's not the best choice for the family room. If there is only one area of your home where you let loose and truly express yourself with color, let the family room be it. Unlike the living room, which is a more formal room, the family room is about ease, comfort, and the idea

Cool green walls add polish to a hallways symmetrical furniture arrangement.

35

of "home." Not only should the family room feel appealing for those who live there, as well as reflect the homeowner's lifestyle, it also needs to put guests at ease when they enter the room. This is difficult to do when a family room is all white. If I am in a home with an all-white family room, I am more concerned about what might be on my shoes and being mindful not to touch the walls than feeling at ease. This is not to say an all-white room does not have its place in a home, but a family room is not the best place for this particular type of décor. This room will suffer spills and be used a lot, so decorate with this in mind.

The family room is the place where you can break the rules and take another direction. Bolder colors may work here where they might not work well in the rest of the house. For example, red is one of those colors perfectly suited for family rooms. Red tones convey warmth, and many other colors work well with red; the same thing can be said for blues. Both colors leave the door open for a variety of complementary colors. Enough about what I like though; the most important thing is the color you choose should be what appeals to you. This is where your portfolio of collected pictures can come in handy to guide you. Sort through your magazine clippings and online printouts, and look for the colors that draw you in. Consider where you live and the style of your home. If I were designing a Mediterranean-style home in Florida, I would not use the dark forest green tones that I might use in a Victorian home in woodsy Maine.

Whatever your favorite color may be, unless it's jazzed up with some contrasting colors, it can be really boring. Choose something from the other end of the color spectrum to bring it to life. Brown is a beautiful color that has become popular, yet brown alone can be a bit boring. To make brown work, choose some exciting accents such as aqua, coral, and goldenrod. If you have a beige sofa, make it pop with boldly colored pillows or a bright chenille throw. If you choose to go more neutral in one area, use color and interesting patterns in another to create impact.

Neutral-colored flooring opens up a lot of possibilities for area rugs and upholstery colors. Hardwood flooring is one of the simplest neutrals to work with. If you do have carpeting, while it is true that it can dictate colors, with a little finesse, most colors can work together. If you find yourself with carpet that is a bold blue or deep green, look for items that will tie it together with the rest of the room. Blues can easily go toward beach style using sand colors and white. Greens benefit from neutrals as well as yellow, pale blue, and certain shades of red, all of which are great color schemes for any room.

A bold red tone conveys warmth in the family room, and there are a number of colors that coordinate perfectly.

Don't be intimidated by color and the wide array of combinations that exist. Instead of thinking of the selection process as overwhelming, think of it as exciting! You get to deign your very own blissful interior, and there are many free resources available to aid you in your selection process. When I find myself veering toward "overwhelming," I will pay a visit to the paint aisle at my local hardware store to see what they put together. You can also explore fabric stores and showrooms. Finding a pattern with your base color mixed with other hues is a trick most designers use to pull together a room's color palette. It will take a lot of the guesswork out of creating a cohesive color palette for your home.

Paint suppliers have come a long way. Look at these sites for colors and inspiration. Yes, they have an app for that! Sites for colors and inspiration:

- Benjaminmoore.com
- Valsparpaint.com
- Glidden.com
- Sherwinwilliams.com
- Housebeautiful.com/decorating/colors/paint-color-ideas
- Bhg.com

Green walls benefit from the use of the neutral colored traditional love seat. Silver accents bring add sparkle and light.

Modern style benefits from the use of color. Even if your scheme is neutral, accents in a red tone keep a space from becoming dull.

CHAPTER 3
LIGHT UP YOUR LIFE

INTERIOR LIGHTING

*"There is one fundamental fact about lighting:
Where there is no light, there is no beauty."*
–Billy Baldwin, *Ruby Ross Wood*

Why do we stumble around in the dark when the solution is so clear? Lighting, like color, furniture, and accessories, is the key to a successful space. Just think what a single light-bulb can do. Then embellish it, control it, and you will never be in the dark again.

Often included as an afterthought, lighting is one of the most important elements in any room and should be the *first* thing you consider after determining your furniture layout. Many newer homes have large family rooms with high ceilings, and because of this, the rooms can seem cavernous. Inadequate lighting in a space such as this detracts from the cozy and inviting feeling a family room should have and can lead to a room feeling stark and cold. The proper use of lighting including dimmers, lamps, and decorative fixtures can easily remedy this feeling.

Show off your style in lighting. A glided gold leaf chandelier provides sparkle and shine, while providing overall illumination for a dining room.

There are three types of lighting to consider when designing your family room—and really any room in your home: general, task, and accent. General lighting refers to overall illumination, the kind that gets lots of everyday use and can light up a room at the flick of a switch. Task lighting serves to illuminate a specific area: a floor lamp next to your favorite reading chair, under-cabinet lights in the kitchen to aid in food preparation, or a desk lamp to prevent eye-strain when balancing the checkbook. Accent lighting works to create mood and highlight areas of visual interest, like picture lights mounted above artwork or a spotlight on a dramatic piece of sculpture. A healthy blend of the three types of lighting will support you in creating a comfortable and beautiful family room where everyone feels right at home.

Table lamps are critical in bringing light to a room, and they are an integral part in a room's overall design.

Illuminate a space gently. Use chandelier shades to cut down on glare, and have multiple light sources to provide even lighting in a room.

One of the best pieces of advice I can give to a person designing a home is to avoid relying on overhead lighting, especially in rooms with high ceilings. Locating lighting near us gives the room a human scale and a sense of comfort. Also remember that just because a room has overhead lighting doesn't mean you are required to use it. Because the goal is to illuminate a room gently, use regular light-bulbs when possible to avoid that sterile supermarket glow that fluorescent bulbs create. The amber light cast from light-bulbs is comforting to most people because the glow is soft, yet practical, and incandescent lamps are dimmable. If you must use fluorescent lighting, look for color-corrected bulbs, or paint the inside of the lampshade pink to create a more subtle glow; you might even consider an opaque shade that reduces the harsh tone of most fluorescent lamps. With fluorescents—especially in lamps—less is more. Go for a lower wattage than you normally would use. This will help in creating a more intimate feeling.

I am a great fan of putting lamps on a table-top dimmer that makes it possible to turn on all your lamps at once. Lowering the lights for a movie night or setting the tone for a get-together is easily done with lights on a dimmer. I also suggest connecting lamps to a wall switch in order to turn them all off or on at the same time. That way, you don't have to walk around the room flipping on and off lamps, and the level of lighting can be controlled by a centralized dimmer.

Hopp Tips:

- Use multiple sources of lighting in all rooms. Overhead lighting should be supplemented with table lamps, desk lamps and accent lighting. Make sure you cover all tasks of the room, working, reading, dining or napping.

- Transform a boring down light to a hanging light fixture using a recessed light conversion kit. Look for them online. It takes only minutes and the result is impressive.

- Install LED puck lights and use them anywhere you can use a little drama. They are perfect under kitchen cabinets for additional lighting, or as back lighting for an interesting object.

- Use a picture light for artwork if there are no accent down lights in the ceiling. Choose a calm finish like bronze or pewter and avoid brass. Picture lights create drama – and they can serve as a nightlight.

- Use dimmers on everything. Use table top dimmers to control lamps, connect them together so they can all be switched on at once. Wall dimmers for down lights not only help to eliminate glare, they are instrumental in creating the perfect mood for a room.

- If you are remodeling, add wall sconces instead of down lights. Lighting from sconces is more pleasant and feels homier.

- Belacor.com
- Shadesoflight.com
- Lampsplus.com
- Potterybarn.com
- Restorationhardware.com
- Lampsusa.com
- Randallwhitehead.com –
  Residential Lighting: A practical Guide

Selecting a lamp for any room shouldn't be an afterthought but rather an integral part in your overall design. What lamps are the right scale, style, and function for a specific location? Look at your design file again to get some knowledge of what works, and then go shopping. In the past, I have purchased very expensive lamps for clients where the price of the shade alone would make you faint. Not anymore! My own home uses lamps from flea markets, antique stores, Pottery Barn, and Target. One of my favorite tricks is to switch my lampshades when I've grown tired of a look instead of replacing the entire lamp. You'd be amazed at how instrumental a lampshade can be in creating a certain style or mood. Lamps are the accessory that aids in establishing a room's personality. They are like the jewelry you add to your favorite outfit to finish a look. Experiment with lampshades, and treat them as you would a piece of furniture. Consider different types of shades: A black lampshade creates drama; a patterned shade adds texture; and colored shades can pull a color scheme together. No matter what you choose, don't be afraid to experiment, and realize that great lighting can be magical.

Lamps are like the jewelry you add to an outfit to finish a look. Use patterned shades for texture and drama.

A weathered flea market lamp is given new life with a silk box-pleated shade. Use a table top dimmer to keep the brightness the way you like it.

PART TWO
ROOMS TO GROW

Now that we have covered some basics, let's move room by room, and discover the professional secrets designers use to transform interiors. Remember that it doesn't have to be expensive. Some of the simplest things, when used well, can create drama and transform a room. Keep an open mind, and make sure you start that design file. It is an important resource to use with this book!

CHAPTER 4
ROOM FOR THE WHOLE FAMILY

THE FAMILY ROOM

"The family is a haven in a heartless world."
–Christopher Lasch

In recent years, the family room has become the heart of the home. It is the first place we go to in order to unwind at the end of the work-day and the last one we leave when retiring at night. There is nothing quite as comforting as coming home, kicking back, and nestling into your favorite spot. You know the one, the space where you feel free just to "be," where it's safe to let go of the stresses of your day, put up your feet, and forget about using a coaster.

The family room's importance has grown through the years, replacing the living room as the home's official gathering place. It's the favorite room in many households—and for good reason. Sometimes used for a quiet night of watching movies and eating popcorn, and other times relied upon for hosting casual gatherings, this is the room that does it all. Whether you call it the den, the gathering room, or simply the family room, this is the room that's all about comfort.

Most often the family room is found adjacent to the kitchen. In newer construction, there is typically no visual divider between the two, creating a "great room" with enough space and functionality for the entire family to assemble. Family rooms tend to be located at the back of the house and provide access to the backyard or outdoor patio area, making this a high-traffic area used by the whole family.

When designing, I aim for creating a casual and inviting space with the intention of bringing people together to enjoy each other's company. Entertainment is the first priority, closely followed by comfortable furnishings, which help to transform an ordinary room into a restful refuge. The two must work in harmony to make a successful family room. Although it is a gathering place for family, we also extend an invitation to our guests to take it easy and be with us. Because of this, it is just as important that the room is comfortable as well as functional. I never sacrifice one for the other. If you've ever had the misfortune of visiting a home with a state-of-the-art television and surround sound speakers, yet with nowhere to sit except on an awkward sofa slung so low that you had to crane your neck to see the TV, you know what I mean. To accomplish a level of comfort while keeping the room useful, there are a number of key design elements to consider.

Two red microfiber sofas are an inexpensive and practical seating solution and will stand up to kids and dogs. The sisal area rug is an environmentally friendly choice in a family room that works well due to its neutral color it's one of the most resilient materials available.

PLAN AHEAD

Creating a functional floor plan is the first step in designing a wonderful family room. If the furniture placement is done poorly, the entire room will suffer, no matter how beautiful the items in the room may be. Often the architecture dictates how furniture should be placed. The architecture indicates to us where to focus our attention in a room. This is called a focal point. Common family room focal points include the television, fireplace, a dominant architectural feature, or even a pleasant view of the outdoors. In today's homes, there is frequently a split focal point: the fireplace and/or the television. Because we can't ignore the architecture of a room, it is important to decide what is really important, and what the true focus of the room should be. If your family room is dominated by a large media wall and your lifestyle is more suited toward watching the game on TV rather than cuddling in front of the fireplace for cocoa and story time, then it's clear which feature is the focal point in your family room. This is not to suggest that other focal points, such as a dramatic architectural detail or a pretty view of the gardens, should be ignored, but rather the main focus becomes our starting point for furniture arrangement. I like to encourage people to experiment with furniture placement. Roll up your sleeves and start shuffling your furniture around until you find the layout that suits you best. Remember, there are many guidelines, but no hard and fast rules. It's all about what works best for you!

The focal point of the bookcases complements the large screen and exemplifies how to achieve a balanced look with asymmetrical placement.

LET'S GO SHOPPING

Once you have established a floor plan, the next step is to choose your furniture. One of the most important purchases made for the family room is the sofa or main seating. Placing the sofa in the room gives immediate fulfillment because it makes the room instantly usable. The sofa or seating is also a strong indicator of the overall design direction of the room. There are many options for furniture, so it is important to hone in on the look you want, and be open to spending more to purchase a quality item that fits your desired look. You shouldn't be afraid to invest in an item if your plan is only to buy it once. Decide if the purchase you are making is trendy, or if it is something you can happily live with for a long time. Although you may love that aqua-colored leather couch today, it may not be the best purchase for the long haul.

It's necessary to be open to different types of seating. All too often people buy family room furniture as a set with a matching couch, love seat, and coffee table coming together in one package. The look is stagnant and boring. To create more visual interest, I suggest purchasing items separately. A great sofa paired with a unique set of chairs or chaise lounge is an opportunity to move away from that "packaged" look and into defining your own style. Additionally, the more seating options, the better! The family room is the place where people go to nestle in or stretch out. There are times when the whole family will want to pile together onto the couch,

Hopp Tips:

- Before you purchase anything else, buy the best sofa you can afford. Not only is this where you sit most of your time, it sets the tone for the room. All the other furniture will fall into place.

- Use the largest coffee table that will work in the room. In the family room you need space to spread out. Avoid delicate finishes that scratch easily and you will worry less.

- Changing a lamp shade is the fastest makeover for a tired lamp. Change the harp size. That way you can size the shade to the lamp. Consider using a black shade – they are very dramatic and create beautiful pools of light.

- No matter how crowded you think your place is a bench always works. Try one on the opposite side of the coffee table, in front of the fireplace or in a hallway. Experiment with your personal style.

- Use a patterned carpet instead of plain. Don't be afraid of pattern. You can use more than you think.

Start creating your personal style. These sites are great for furniture, lighting, rugs, art and accessories:

- Homedecorators.com
- Aaronbrothers.com
- Ballarddesigns.com
- Grandinroad.com
- Wisteria.com
- Highfashionhome.com
- Pier1.com
- Lampsplus.com
- Theshadestore.com

and other times when someone wants to cozy into the corner of an oversized chair alone. Seating options will allow this to happen. When you buy pieces individually, you have more liberty to create a layout that works for your personality and lifestyle.

Regardless of the style, two key factors to consider when choosing seating are comfort and durability. Fortunately, price doesn't dictate either. I have sat on some very expensive couches that have left my back aching and some very affordable ones that were amazingly comfortable. No one wants to sit on a chair or sofa that isn't comfortable no matter how great it looks, nor do you want a guest stuck sitting in that one chair you know your family doesn't like to use. You also don't want to have to worry constantly about spills or usage when it comes to family room seating. The family room is a high-traffic area. It is meant to be used, and you can expect it to get a little beat-up, so when choosing your sofa, think about the fabric you want covering it.

Flanked by standing lamps, the Ralph Lauren style love seat sized sofa is the right scale on a small wall. Dark wood pieces provide a fresh contrast to white walls. Casual accesories in asymmetrical arrangements maintain the laid-back feeling of the room.

I once had a client who wanted a white sofa in her family room. She didn't have children, so she wasn't concerned about the spills and stains that growing kids inevitably create. She did, however, love to host parties big and small and frequently open her home to guests. I gently reminded her that children aren't the only ones to occasionally tip a glass or drop a greasy snack, and that perhaps a white sofa would be better suited for a space like the living room where it won't get as much use.

If you know people will be eating in the family room, don't purchase delicate pale cotton that quickly absorbs stains. One idea that is rapidly becoming popular is using outdoor fabrics for upholstery. Consisting of acrylic, these fabrics are not only fade resistant, but you can actually use bleach to clean them. The fabric is extremely durable, and in recent years, manufacturers have developed softer weaves such as chenille or velvet that don't feel like the outdoor canvas most of us remember.

Rust-colored stars create a memorable focal point on an expansive wall. The denim slip covered sofa, along with pine pieces complete the cozy, casual vibe. Brightly colored hydrangeas are my favorite flower in any setting.

Choose the largest coffee table that will fit comfortably in a room. Choose a design that works well with your family's lifestyle.

One of my favorite touches for family rooms is using the largest coffee table the room and arrangement will allow. The rule for the coffee table is that its placement is no more than 12 to 18 inches from the edge of the sofa or chair. This is so you can reach it without stretching, or if you prefer, it's a good distance so you can put your feet up. Big coffee tables serve to bring people together. They are a place to sit for an impromptu TV dinner, or gather around for a night of games. Your favorite books and magazines can be placed there with room to spread out. Like the sofa, the coffee table is an important element in setting the style and direction of the room. It continues the layering process of the complete design.

When selecting the coffee table, it is important to consider your family's lifestyle first and foremost. Those with little ones running around may want to avoid tables with sharp corners. If you have pets that climb on the furniture, it may be wise to find a table without a glass top that would require constant cleaning. For families who like to park it in front of the TV with a take-out dinner, a high-gloss finish that scratches easily won't be the best option either. Calculate how you will use the table. Generally, I opt for vintage tables with a bit more character—and because they already have scratches! The family room is the last place one should have to worry about being careful.

Another one of my favorites is to use an upholstered ottoman as a coffee table. This has become immensely popular recently with many designs that offer storage as well. The advantage of the ottoman is the casual feeling it implies. It practically asks you to put your feet up and relax. Bear in mind that you will need a tray to set things on—which is another expression of your style. From silver to rattan, the tray is a functional accessory that can be changed easily and ultimately makes an upholstered ottoman far more practical.

Design tip: Find a swanky vinyl fabric for the upholstered ottoman instead of leather. Vinyl is far more stain resistant and holds up better. And you can rest a little better knowing that little hands leaving sticky peanut butter prints will clean up with minimal effort.

Hopp Tips:

- Electronics should be heard and not seen. If you can't afford to update your electronics, keep them hidden in a cabinet or closet. Get an infrared remote and receiver so you can control the av system while keeping the cabinet doors closed. Radio Shack and electronic stores sell them.

- Buy throw blankets for different seasons. Heavier weights and richer colors for winter, and lighter weight and lighter colors for summer months.

- Buy woven grass shades for your windows. They cut down on the harshest sun during day light and can insulate your home from cold drafts. They work in almost any interior and visually warm a room.

- Upholster an ottoman with an old rug. That way you can use a time worn carpet in a completely new way. Don't worry about the pattern repeat. The design stands on its own.

- Create a picture wall. Buy 10 frames of the same finish in varying sizes. Be sure to buy matting for all the frames for a custom look. Print your favorite family or vacation photos in black and white or sepia. Instant art gallery!

PUT IT AWAY

The next essential consideration for the family room is storage. While this room is usually about media, these items can take up space and cause the room to look messy. Again, because this is a room for the family to use and relax in, it is important to get rid of the "psychological noise" caused by clutter. Face it. People feel better when the surroundings are tidy. When CDs, books, toys, and other items are everywhere, it is harder to feel at ease. Look for items that make it possible to put things away easily. For example, if your lifestyle supports it, consider buying a coffee table or ottoman that also has a functional storage space. If you are someone who enjoys scrapbooking or another hobby that involves a lot of items, find a chest or cabinet where these items can quickly be stored away and also be easily brought out again. Purchase inexpensive baskets for storing children's toys, or select bookcases with doors over some of the shelves to hide DVDs and video games. When incorporating bookcases, it is best to consider them not so much as storage but as display.

Bookcases are a wonderful feature that can create a laid-back library feel and look best when they are not crammed full of stuff. The use of baskets for hobby items as mentioned above or books mixed with family photos and special art pieces or collections are all important ways of keeping bookcases functional and neat looking. Step back and look at the shelves; do you need everything there? Are the items important? Do you like the way they are arranged? If not, edit out the bad, and keep only the stuff that makes you feel good when nesting in this important space. Remember the goal is to *put away the clutter*! More about bookcases in the living room section!

A neutral colored sofa is boldly paired with patterned lounge chairs. Wicker suitcases serve as convenient side tables while providing additional storage. Baskets aid in keeping the bookcases organized while vintage clocks, an armillary and antique mirror complete the vintage chic look of this family room.

CHAPTER 5
WHAT'S COOKING?

THE KITCHEN

"In the childhood memories of every good cook, there's a large kitchen, a warm stove, a simmering pot and a mom."
–Barbara Costikyan

LOVE THE ONE YOU ARE WITH

Having a beautiful kitchen is not about status. It is about having a space you truly love. It's about usable workspace, good lighting, functional layout, and another place to enjoy in your home. Just looking at the number of design magazines focused on kitchen design will tell you that the popularity of kitchens has come a long way in the last 50 years. Take a look at new homes being built and you will see the kitchen/family room arrangement is the most important of the house. Granite counters, center islands, and stainless steel appliances are the new standard. This chapter is about personalizing your kitchen for your taste and lifestyle regardless of whether you have a newly built property or a previously owned home. Use these tips and tricks to create a space that makes you want to cook!

Sometimes what we want and what our budget says we can have aren't one and the same. Luckily, there are many ways to achieve interior bliss and create the look you want without going overboard and over budget. If your kitchen is in need of an update, and you don't have the funds for a full remodel, don't fret. I'll share with you some of my secrets for revamping and revitalizing this important room in your home.

Neatness counts in a small kitchen! Put everything away that you don't use daily, and keep items on the countertop to a minimum. In this eclectic kitchen, vintage accessories are an ideal accompaniment to the transitional style of the cabinets.

GET OUT THE PAINT-BRUSH

In an existing kitchen, one of the most dramatic, cost-effective, and easy changes is paint. When I say "easy," I mean if you hire someone else to paint! If you are a good do-it-yourselfer, it is a lot of work but well worth the results. Paint immediately makes anything look fresher and cleaner. The color selection, however, should be coordinated with the overall style you want for the room. From simple off-white to a slick high gloss or a painted and sanded rustic finish, the choice you make is one of the most important in achieving your design. This is why I suggest you have a design file that holds the looks, features, and designs you like. This is an important reference that is uniquely yours. When decisions need to be made, it is an invaluable tool.

When approaching the color selection, consider how much is wall space and how much is cabinet, counters, and backsplash. The amount of daylight and overhead lighting is an important factor as well. I generally advise not to use dark colors on the kitchen walls. Of course it depends on the situation. In small kitchens, dark colors can make the room feel even smaller. Nevertheless, a

67

darker color will create a greater sense of drama. Whatever you choose, it should be reviewed at different times of the day and with lights on and off. I once painted a client's living room cottage white, which is a beautiful creamy white. A few days later, the client called me and said she thought there was too much green in the color. Cottage white is a color I use quite often, and there is definitely no green in it. It turns out that during the day, the woman had her drapery open, and the light reflected off the greenery in the yard and changed the appearance of the paint color on the walls. That was an invaluable lesson that I have not forgotten to this day. Paints change color all the time depending on the light source. This is why when choosing a color, it is important to see a sample color on more than one wall, at different times of day, and definitely with the primary light source on and off.

One of the goals of hiring a designer is to have ideas presented that you wouldn't otherwise come across. A lot of people don't consider painting their cabinets, especially if they are a solid wood such as oak. Why not? The cabinets are one of the largest surfaces in the room and the most important in establishing

Hopp Tips:

- Find attractive canisters for items on the kitchen counter. There is no rule that says that they can't be the same size. For a finished look, coordinate them with a matching tray.

- Change out all your kitchen cabinetry hardware. Go for a style more suitable to your kitchen's interior. I love old fashioned glass knobs. Bronze is my other favorite finish.

- Get a brightly colored mixer for your kitchen. Kitchenaid has colors from Cobalt to Cinnamon. Even if you don't bake, it's a colorful icon for the kitchen. And the only appliance that should be on your counters.

- For a smart centerpiece get some nice wicker baskets or bowls. Group them together and fill them with apples, oranges and walnuts. Change it seasonally. It's stylish and you can eat it too!

- Create a kitchen island from stainless steel shelving from Metro shelves. Add a stone slab or butcher block to make the top.

Trays are not only a smart way to keep kitchen counters organized, they camouflage mismatched pitchers bottles and other items.

your look. For example, if you want to go for a more beach-like look, choose off-white, and use accents in a sea green or marine blue. A more contemporary look benefits from a bold color in high gloss or a darker color like espresso. This works particularly well on flat-panel doors. Another direction may be a distressed or glazed finish that welcomes a more casual urban country feeling. There have been so many oak cabinets installed during the last three decades that they tend to date the kitchen, especially if they have yellowed over time. Paint them, and you open up a world of possibilities. Just remember to do the prep work when painting wood. You want to make sure you get a good-looking finish that lasts a long time.

Don't overlook kitchen hardware. Even though cabinet knobs aren't necessary with many cabinet doors these days, adding knobs is easier than painting. Knobs and pulls are another important detail in creating your look. If your house has a traditional style or has the look of a historic home, adding glass knobs go far in complementing that style. Glass knobs come in a number of colors, so you will find a color that works with both lighter and darker finished cabinets. In more contemporary kitchens with stainless steel appliances, consider brushed nickel. Oil-rubbed bronze and painted bronze are particularly beautiful. The finish on oil-rubbed will wear down

with use to a lighter tone that looks more antique, so be prepared for that change. Painted bronze is a more durable finish and doesn't have the same problem. I have seen all these styles of knobs and pulls sold at basic hardware stores and furniture stores such as Pottery Barn and Restoration Hardware.

When deciding which knobs to use, go to a hardware store and purchase several different types. Take them home, hold them up to your cabinets, and decide which one you like the most. Take the rejects back to the store when you go to buy the winning selection. I do this with clients. Even for the best designers, design isn't a process where it just happens. Rarely is it something where a product can be brought in, and the process is done. Sometimes choosing something as simple as cabinet door knobs can seem agonizing because what might seem perfect in the store often isn't when you get it home.

New knobs change the look of kitchen cabinets in an instant, and they are easy to install.

69

CLEAR THE CLUTTER

Command central is in the kitchen. The last century has seen kitchens go from the rear private area of a house to the new standard with the kitchen that opens to a family room, making it the busiest part of the house that welcomes family and friends. Since the kitchen has become a much more important space, it has also become the place where stuff collects. The challenge is keeping all that stuff in check. For example, how often do you really use your toaster or blender? Do small appliances really need to be on the counter all the time? Most of us also keep items we may use a lot or just think we need on the counters. When did we start featuring kitchen utensils? Put them away in a drawer. They do not add anything to the overall look, and they never look tidy.

A Rwandan basket and cheery mums are bright accessories against a neutral backsplash.

The counters are claimed by bottles of vitamins, a box for mail, canisters, fire extinguishers, recyclables, and more. Simply taking these things off the counters and keeping only the essentials needed for everyday use can transform a kitchen. The fewer items on the counters, the tidier your kitchen looks. Instead of placing appliances on the counter, find something decorative. While the toaster might fit into that space just as easily, a decorative piece is much nicer to look at than an appliance.

However, there are some items that families want to have readily available on the counter. The idea is to find ways to make them part of the overall look, rather than part of the clutter. For example, canisters holding coffee, flour, sugar, and other items are commonly found on the kitchen counters in many homes. If you choose to have them, use them decoratively. Choose wisely to add to the style of your kitchen. If you have clear canisters, consider putting interesting items in them, like colorful pasta, oats, beans, or something else people wouldn't expect. Instead of leaving the liquid dish or hand soap in its plastic container, put it in a decorative pump. It's a way to get the ugly bottle off the counter but keep the soap handy. Place sponges and scrubbies in a cute ceramic bowl or wire basket. This keeps the sink area neat, and also corrals our "stuff" into something that is part of the décor.

When designers and stagers furnish a kitchen, they do not go for toasters and coffeemakers; they bring in decorative items. Look in your kitchen to see where the eye naturally goes. Look for corners or unusual spaces. For example, if you have a microwave mounted above a counter, place something in that space below. One suggestion is a tray of vinegar or oil bottles. These can be found at stores like Marshalls or Ross, and they are filled with herbs, fruits, or vegetables to add color to an area. Another idea is using decorative plates. They can be hung on the wall or placed in a plate stand. These are items that can be used as decorative accessories, but they also make the home look lived in.

Another idea is to use the backsplash area to hang art. Since this is a low area, many people do not think of using this space for decorating. However, a vintage sign can add some play to a country kitchen, while a modern black-and-white still life of fruit can add a bit of drama to the contemporary kitchen.

Many newer homes have a built-in kitchen desk, and if not, almost all homes have what I call the "kitchen office." This is where the phone and answering machine are placed. Bills might pile up there. Some people may even have a computer set up. This is also an area that sees a lot of clutter. One way to keep that clutter manageable is to purchase an organizer. There are some beautiful designs made of wood or woven grass that can help control the mess and add to the look of the kitchen. If you don't want an organizer, try a unique tray or

Choose colorful canisters—they are practical storage that spice up a kitchen counter.

baskets with lids for these things. They will keep items contained and help you to keep items more organized.

Also, add items to the kitchen desk to help define the space and dress it up a little. For example, purchase a small lamp for the area. As I mentioned earlier, lamps are perfect accessories for dressing up a room. Add a bulletin board. There are great fabric-covered ones, and since this area is usually away from where the cooking takes place, there should not be any problem about it getting dirty or splattered. Have small boxes or baskets available to place miscellaneous items in. When you look at design magazines, everything is tidy, but we all know real life happens—so allow it. Thinking about how to keep things tidy will save you from headaches later. For one, you will always be able to find things, but also when things are tidy, people tend to feel better.

Check out these sites that are useful for updating the kitchen and breakfast room:

- Potterybarn.com
- Bedbathandbeyond.com
- Myknobs.com
- Countryliving.com
- Kitchens.com

Bronze light fixtures set the tone for this updated traditional kitchen. Since it opens to the family room, it's important to keep the counters clear and clutter to a minimum. Greens on the windowsill add freshness to any kitchen. Whether live or artificial, change plants seasonally to keep your look up to date.

FANTASY ISLAND

The kitchen island is one of the best changes to come along in decades. A large open work surface that serves as home gathering spot—how did we do without it? As a focal point in most kitchens, keep it clear. It's command central, not clutter island. If you need to put things on the island because you just have to use them, place them in a tray. Silver, wooden, and rattan trays are options that are best as they are either easy to clean or easily replaced at little cost.

A kitchen island is a fantastic way to expand your counter space, add seating, and even add appliances like a second sink or oven. More counter space can also mean more opportunity for clutter, so keep it in check and avoid having it become another space for your stuff. Let the island become another place to imprint your personal style, and take your kitchen to the next level of fabulous. Keep in mind whatever you place on your island must be easy to move. Since the island is a place where work happens, the decorative items on it can't be extra heavy or unwieldy. One of the best suggestions I have for an island is to place a big bowl of fruit on it. A bowl of oranges or apples adds color to a room, and the fruit becomes an inexpensive decorative accessory you can eat! Plus, it's easy to change your accessory as often as you like; just add it onto the weekly grocery list.

Painting the island a color different from the rest of the kitchen cabinets is my favorite way to make the island stand out and up the wow factor. You can get away with doing this because the island can function as a piece of furniture, and there's no rule that says it has to match everything else. In fact, with furniture, it's best to utilize different colors and finishes to keep a room appealing and interesting. If the rest of your kitchen is white, consider painting the island black or another color that breaks away from the monotony of the other surfaces.

Another way to spice up the island and add to the overall look of the kitchen is to install hanging lights above the island. Lighting above the island is an opportunity to express or enhance the style you are going for, and the right style of lighting can help transform a room because it becomes part of the architecture. These pendants can be either a simple fixture with a cord and a glass diffuser or metal rods with a more decorative shade. One problem many people run into is the current energy codes. Many builders place fluorescent lighting in homes for day-to-day lighting to meet these codes, which is fine. Unfortunately, fluorescent lighting usually isn't very pretty, and at night, people don't usually want or need that much light. If you can get around the fluorescent lights, your pendant lights will cast a beautiful glow in the kitchen, make the room appear homier, and provide enough light to move about the kitchen safely to get a drink of water or grab a snack.

The kitchen is a great place for displaying art and accessories, and you don't have to limit yourself to the typical kitchen art of forks and spoons. Decorative items on the counters should be easy to move when you need to use the space for food preparation.

Keep it simple in a small breakfast room. Use decorative trays to stay organized. Feel free to mix and match different items to keep things visually interesting.

DINING IN

Separate from the dining room, many homes have an eat-in kitchen or a breakfast area. Today, this is usually where most people eat rather than gathering in a formal dining room. While the breakfast area should continue to express the main look of the house, it is important that the design from the rest of the kitchen carry over into this area. If your family does most eating in this area, be sure to choose comfortable seating. Also, since these chairs will get a lot of wear and tear, make sure they can be easily cleaned. If you choose to have cloth-covered seating, purchase chairs with a removable seat cushion so they can be easily laundered or replaced if necessary. Or choose indoor/outdoor fabric that can take a beating and be scrubbed. I like how something as simple as a seat cushion can finish off an area. If your kitchen is styled in a country motif, you may want a cheerful gingham fabric. The fabric doesn't necessarily have to be the same for all seating throughout the entire kitchen. If you have barstools in the kitchen, cover them in a complementary striped or floral pattern to match the country gingham in the breakfast area.

Feel free to mix and match materials and colors as well as fabrics in the kitchen and breakfast area. The more you mix, the more attractive and visually appealing your eat-in kitchen will become. You may choose to have wooden chairs in the breakfast room and wicker barstools along the long counter in your kitchen. There are many ways to play with seating to make it part of an overall look. In a client's kitchen, we used a long bench on one side of the table and chairs on the other. This combination worked and was interesting and unexpected.

As with the kitchen island, an easy way to update the breakfast room is to change the light fixture. Developers tend to choose cheap light fixtures. While there's no problem with cheap, there is a very big problem with looking cheap. There are a multitude of better looks available, so if your budget allows it, consider changing the light fixture above the kitchen table. Pottery Barn has online sales virtually all the time, and the looks they offer are consistent with what is currently happening stylewise and tend to be timeless. Lamps Plus has a terrific online store with a huge selection, offering solutions for every budget and style. One thing to keep in mind if you have pendant lights above the island is that the lighting in the breakfast area should coordinate with it. It doesn't have to be the same design, but it should share some commonalities such as the same finish or same glass. It's all in how you mix it up!

WINDOW SHOPPING

Capitalize on your kitchen windows by treating them as another facet of your kitchen design. All too often, windows are simply overlooked. They should continue to establish your look while carrying that style over to your breakfast room or eat-in kitchen. Before choosing window treatments, think about what you need them to do and how they will work with your design scheme. If light control is important, look for materials such as woven grass blinds that can filter excessive light. If light control is not an issue, you may only need to use a valance or light curtains. One client I worked with used vintage-looking hand towels. She transformed them into fabulous curtains by placing a seam across the top and then just let them hang. While it was an inexpensive and creative way to dress the windows, that one small touch completed the shabby chic look of her adorable kitchen.

In addition to thinking about your kitchen window coverings, it is important to keep the windowsills clean and free of clutter. Remember that this is a place where food is prepared, and cleanliness is a top priority. Keep the tchotchkes off the windowsill to eliminate the buildup of dust and grime and to keep the kitchen looking fresh and neat.

STARTING FROM SCRATCH

There is much joy to be found in designing your own kitchen. Whether your budget is big or small, it is possible to have the kitchen of your dreams by knowing where to scrimp and where to spend. If you have got to choose between the best appliances and custom cabinetry, my advice is to get the best appliances you can afford. They will pay you back in the long run, and with ready-made cabinets coming in such a variety of styles these days, you can often achieve the look you want for less than you think.

Right now stainless steel appliances are all the rage, and they are very likely to continue ruling the top spot for kitchen appliance finishes, but that does not mean you have to have stainless steel, especially if it is not within your budget or part of your design scheme. I suggest looking at different styles of appliances that will add to your overall design. There are new appliances that appear vintage and others that look very contemporary and modern. Consider all the options in terms of color and style within your price range before making a decision. It does not matter that the Joneses have stainless steel; you do not need to keep up with them! In fact, once they see your super sleek white refrigerator and range-top stove, they just might want white too.

Choosing the right type of flooring for your lifestyle is another important consideration when designing a kitchen. In any high-traffic area, such as the kitchen, and especially in an eating area, I strongly suggest tile or wood. I very, very rarely put a rug in a breakfast area. It is hard to maintain cleanliness, and the rug prevents chairs from moving easily. If you would like a rug placed somewhere, put it in front of the sink or opt for runners (long narrow rugs) on each side of the island. Since the kitchen floor requires frequent cleaning, forgo the rug if you can; otherwise, consider getting two—one to keep on the floor while the other is in the washing machine.

Colorful flowers, apothecaries with fruit and bright yellow ceramics bring important color to this striking kitchen.

Use the kitchen backsplash as a gallery of your collections. If you are afraid to drill into tile, use plate stands, double stick tape or Velcro to attach to the wall.

When faced with deciding what to do with the countertops, get ready to pay up. It truly pays to invest in good countertops. It is far better to have solid stone counters paired with an inexpensive backsplash than a cheap counter surface and an expensive backsplash. Consider how much wear and tear from chopping and cutting to spilling and grilling your counters face every day. Kitchen counters endure a lot of abuse, and the higher-grade materials not only look better, they also stand the test of time. Believe me, making a one-time investment in good kitchen countertops is a lot less expensive than having to replace chipped and cracked counters in the future.

If your budget allows it, under-cabinet lighting is a brilliant way to add a little luxury to your kitchen, and luxury that is useful as well. Under-cabinet lighting is becoming more and more common in newer homes, and if you have the opportunity to add it, do it. Under-cabinet lighting is important because it casts light in an area that would otherwise be dark. The light creates a warm glow, and when paired with pendant lights above the island, the layering effect is quite beautiful. If you cannot afford under-cabinet lights right now, there is a clever little solution called puck lights. They are small round lights with an adhesive backing. Some are even battery powered. Puck lights can be placed at intervals under your existing cabinets. Really, there is no reason to turn on the harsh light of the overheads except when cleaning or trying to get guests to leave at the end of the evening. Also, it is impossible to dim fluorescents, while a dimmer can be used with incandescent lights like the pendants over the island.

Whether starting a kitchen from scratch or enhancing what you already have, it is important to remember that the kitchen is about form and function. Make sure your kitchen meets all your space and layout needs, so that you can prepare food, serve quick meals, and prepare 100 brownies for tomorrow's bake sale and create an atmosphere that makes guests feel welcome to sit and chat over a cup of coffee.

Kitchen islands provide needed work surfaces. A bowl of fruit is an inexpensive accessory that adds color that you can eat.

CHAPTER 6
MAKE EVERY ROOM
A *LIVING* ROOM

THE LIVING AND DINING ROOMS

"The living room should be a place where we feel totally at ease – temple of the soul."
–Terence Conran

I grew up in a 1940s Cape Cod style of house that my parents remodeled a number of times to accommodate eight children. We were one of the rare families that actually used the living room—probably because there was nowhere else to sit! Plus, we didn't have a family room. I remember visiting a friend's house that had a very elegant living room with white carpeting and powder blue furniture. It was the height of style! Yet no one used it. It was like a trophy that people admired as they went past it into the rest of the house. They might as well have roped it off and charged admission. I remember that room to this day because it seemed so silly not to use it. Living rooms were meant for living. However, as the family room increased in popularity, the living room has become somewhat obsolete. We may never overcome the family room's power as the primary living space, yet we can create an inviting place where you can gather with friends and they don't have to feel guarded and uncomfortable.

One of my primary tasks when staging homes was to make a house inviting. That included the living room, of course, and I created spaces that were chic, inviting, and comfortable. The key was to show people how they could live in the space. My job was to help potential buyers visualize their life in this house or apartment.

STAY IN FOCUS

One of the first things to do when decorating the living room is choosing a focal point. Usually the focal point is one of three things: a fireplace; a view, either out the window or to another space; or the room's architecture, which can be something like built-in bookcases or some other feature. The idea of a focal point is to create focus, the visual or dramatic center that all the furniture is gathered around and becomes the room's core. Walking into this room should evoke a sense of ease and comfort. Why create a beautiful room that is never used? Instead, bring in furniture, art, and accessories that will make you happy and literally invite everyone to come in and enjoy the space.

For example, when using the fireplace as the focal point, use something creative that draws people in and entertains the eye. One technique is asymmetrical balance. This could be achieved by placing a mirror above the mantel and then placing a few tall candlesticks on one side and a sculpture or floral arrangement on the other. The items aren't matching, yet they still create a sense of symmetry. Another idea is to center art above the mantel and use a series of plants or flowers in terra-cotta pots below. This is a striking composition. Remember to change the flowers seasonally or use an artificial arrangement as mentioned previously. Dead plants do not make anyone feel comfortable.

I see no reason why you should not have a television in the living room if that will make you use the room more. However, you should avoid having the TV become the focal point because electronics are generally not that attractive. Avoid hanging a flat-panel TV above the mantel if you can. Unlike the family room, this space isn't all about television. Look for an alternative, such as a cabinet or side-wall, if that will work with your furniture grouping.

The focal point of this living room is the antique cabinet that houses the television and media equipment while the drawers provide convenient storage.

This stylish, contemporary, and eclectic furniture collection is a brilliant solution for this small-scale living room. The clock on the mantle serves as a focal point, making the room appear deeper. Modern and ethnic accessories bring the room to life and round out the space, without making it feel cluttered.

HAVE A SEAT

Generally, the sofa is the first piece purchased and is the primary indicator of the room's direction. A more casual sofa makes people feel relaxed. If you prefer a more formal look, avoid purchasing pieces that all match. The best formal spaces mix upholstery, wood, and iron in an eclectic mix that is far more exciting. Regardless of the selection, when buying the sofa, consider the other pieces that will work with it. For example, a more laid-back striped sofa is easily paired with woven reed chairs in a patterned fabric and an old chest or picnic table as a coffee table. If your preference is more formal, a linen sofa and mismatched chairs and crystal lamps are a perfect combination. Look for ways to make the room more inviting through the use of ottomans, brightly colored pillows, art, plants, books, and accessories. There are a number of sofa styles; it's the complementary pieces that establish a room's atmosphere.

Choose the sofa first and make sure to select one that is comfortable. Make the room inviting through the use of bright pillows, art, plants, books and accessories.

Perfect symmetry was created by the sofa centered on the fireplace and the arrangement of the four cane chairs. This grouping provides ample seating, while still allowing room to circulate. Supplementing the fireplace's mantle, a classically inspired fretwork mirror adds a bit of elegance, while the Chinese tables flanking the fireplace maintain the room's casual atmosphere.

Once the sofa is nailed down, start filling in. Chairs are the next item for the room, and there are a multitude of styles you can use. Rooms that have everything match are boring, so be creative. A beat-up French armchair with a plush wing chair and an upholstered lounge chair can all work together beautifully. Also, do not get stuck in "period" looks. I like to upholster old antique pieces in something unexpected like pony skin, wide stripes, or bold colors. Look at your inspiration photos, and you will see different scales, varying ages, and a mixture of fully upholstered or wood frame chairs with painted or stained finishes. Remember, fabric is more than just for upholstery. For example, a skirted table is a trick I use frequently—not so much to hide anything as to introduce softness, color, and interest.

The seating arrangement doesn't need to be traditional either. Pull the sofa away from the wall and float it in the room. Create different seating areas using tables and chairs. A client of mine had an arrangement that was two sofas centered on a fireplace, which is a perfectly acceptable thing to do. I pulled them apart to the opposite ends of the room, gave each different coffee and end tables, and added assorted chairs in each vignette. We repurposed an old ottoman and upholstered it with the better parts of a fraying Oriental rug. The ottoman in front of the fireplace became the focal point, and the other groupings provided far more seating than before, taking advantage of all the room's usable space.

Hopp Tips:

- Buy the seating for the living room first. This will determine the room's layout and it sets the direction for the entire room.

- One way to create a room with a cohesive polished look is by telling a story with accessories. Start with one room and take out all the smaller bits and pieces. Choose one color and weave it throughout the room with vases, pillow, throw and candlesticks. Find a tray (or paint one) the same color and put it on your coffee table.

- Ready made window treatments can be updated with a fabric trim or contrasting border. If you can't find panels long enough, consider buying a second set of panels and use them to add a contrasting color to the bottom or top. If you don't know how to sew, take them to a tailor. It's a snap for them.

- Place a large mirror opposite a window. It will open up the room and double the amount of light.

- Think outside the box when choosing a coffee table. Tables at tea height (22") are more versatile and you can even eat at them. The height creates a different setting that is much more interesting.

TO THE FLOOR

Wall-to-wall carpeting naturally has a large impact on a room's design direction. If you don't love the carpet, pull up a corner, and see what's underneath. If there is hardwood floor, invest in refinishing it; there is nothing like hardwood. If you must keep carpeting, area rugs placed on top are another idea. They can help you define a seating area, and the rug may help camouflage an unattractive carpet. Remember to use rug-to-rug pads to prevent the area rug from creeping and slipping.

There are so many rugs to choose from, it can be overwhelming. This is one of the more important elements in a room because you can add color and pattern on the floor that may not look good on upholstered pieces. Selecting a rug is a process of education. Look online. Go to stores, and if they have a smaller-scale rug that you can buy (and return), it will help you identify which color, pattern, and texture will work best for your space. An important rule with area rugs is that they should be as large as the furniture grouping. The rule tends to be that all furniture is either on or off the rug. While I break that rule occasionally, I suggest that you buy larger rugs. The small ones that only anchor a coffee table never look right. A larger area rug is more dramatic, and you will find that your room can handle a larger one than you may have thought.

One material I like to use for flooring is sisal or sea grass. Sisal is an all-natural woven grass; sea grass is a closed-fiber material that can be softer than sisal. This type of rug has become more common recently, and you can find it at stores such as Target and Pottery Barn. Although sisal would seem to create a casual look, it can easily be incorporated into more formal rooms as a notable departure from what is usually used. I have designed some very elegant formal living rooms that worked perfectly with sisal rugs. There is something about sisal that allows it to complement casual interiors as well as more formal rooms. While sisal is one of the least expensive floor coverings to use, it makes an impact because it rethinks the traditional Oriental rug many expect to see in the living room.

BY THE BOOK

Bookcases are a wonderful way to enhance a living room. Like armoires, bookcases create a vertical balance that keeps the room interesting and are a break from too many horizontal elements. In a more formal look, display collections of ceramics or crystal and, of course, books. More casual rooms can use bookcases for odd finds from your travels, other treasures that do not

The rule with area rugs is that they should be as large as the furniture grouping. It's more dramatic and the room can handle a larger rug than you thought.

In bookcases, keep only the items that are most meaningful to you. Be creative when displaying items and don't be afraid to mix things up.

look formal, as well as books stacked and placed more randomly than you would in a dressier environment. Bookcases make a space appear more livable and inviting. They allow us to organize our things into collections and display items that are important to us. Generally, I tend to avoid using personal or family photos in the living room. Family photos work best in private areas where they can be appreciated. That is why I suggest using them in hallways and bedrooms, and, occasionally, I will work a few into family rooms. Instead, consider unusual artwork that catches your attention and complements the room, whether it is on the walls or on a bookcase shelf.

Each shelf in a bookcase should have books, art, and objects that can be worked in creatively—but get rid of most of the "stuff" and keep only the items that are most beautiful or meaningful. If you have paperbacks, take them out, and only use books with hard bindings. Consider taking the jackets off the books. Often, you'll uncover dramatically colored bindings with embossed lettering. If you don't have enough books, then you can use objects or books on their sides to act as bookends, but be sure to remove any growing collections that are taking over the shelves.

WINDOWS TO THE WORLD

The choice of window treatments depends on the amount of light coming from the windows as well as privacy concerns, just as it does in other parts of the house. To control the light, you may choose wooden blinds or woven-grass shades. If you are using either, consider using decorative side hanging drapery panels. They give the window a more finished look, and the fabric is a great sound absorber. If sunlight isn't a concern, use sheer drapery. In recent years, the look of sheers has been updated, and these days you can easily find them with woven patterns such as vines or geometric designs. Drapery and decorative side panels are a softer look that is almost always perfect for framing a window. I am continually amazed at how draperies change a room and create a sense of warmth.

Living room draperies don't have to be expensive. If you know how to sew, you can save a bundle. If you don't sew, premade drapery panels are available in a multitude of styles and colors. I often look online for inspiration and frequently find exactly what I want. Restoration Hardware has beautiful silk panels. Country Curtains has reasonably priced draperies, valances, and Roman shades. Even JCPenney has custom draperies, although their fabric selections aren't always the best.

This combination finish of black and burnished silver is more interesting than a single finish and the unstructured French pleats offer a more relaxed drapery heading that suits a casual look.

Drapery hardware is the finishing touch for window treatments. The days of the unattractive white metal traversing tracks are over. The only time to use them is when they are hidden by a valance or the architecture. Again, a computer search of drapery hardware will gather a wealth of options from iron to wood. There are even some contemporary hardware designs that use tension wires. I tend to be more of a traditionalist and opt for wooden or iron rods. One way to transform a bland rod is by using finials and rings that are a different finish from the rod and bracket. For example, if you have a dark bronze rod, golden colored rings and finials are a stunning combination. Even if your budget doesn't allow for new hardware, buy spray paint. New paint can transform anything and is a quick fix.

These are some of my favorite sites for furnishings and inspiration. They have a number of things you can add to your design file:

- CrateandBarrel.com
- Laylagrayce.com
- Zgallerie.com
- Mgbwhome.com

- Wisteria.com
- Horchow.com
- Restorationhardware.com
- Overstock.com

Oversized end tables in a living room provide ample space for display. Choose items that agree in scale to create an appealing combination.

LIGHTEN THE MOOD

Lighting is tremendously important in establishing the mood you are creating as well as its more functional qualities. And the living room is no exception. To start, identify the areas where you need additional lighting, and select lamps that complement your style. Lamps are important because they bring lighting to a more human scale. People are most comfortable with lighting at or near their height. Overhead lights are great as long as they are on dimmers. Ideally, if you have recessed lighting, it should focus on an item such as a coffee table, a mantel, or an art piece on the wall. If you have a more typical grid layout, use the lights for a soft ambient glow while using decorative lamps for the primary source of light.

As I mentioned before, a shade is to a lamp as jewelry is to an outfit. Jewelry finishes the outfit, and the shade can make the lamp. Generally, the shades that come with the lamp are pretty boring. Changing lampshades is a remarkably simple trick that can immediately update a lamp. I generally keep it simple by stopping by Pottery Barn or Restoration Hardware. Their styles are current, and the designs are fairly straightforward. From linen to calligraphy to embroidery, the options for lampshades are plentiful. Another resource, of course, is the Internet. Shades of Light has a number of designs that I like, and Lamps Plus has more than a thousand shades. Recently, I did a search for a black lampshade and came up with numerous sites. There is nothing like a black lampshade to add drama!

It seems we never go to the trouble of turning all the lamps on. The solution is to control all the lamps together. This works perfectly if you have a wall switch. Simply use an extension cord to connect all the lamps to the switched outlet. Make sure the wall switch is on a dimmer. If you don't have a wall switch, use a table-top dimmer and connect all the lamps together. Dimmers like this are fairly common now, and there are simple systems that have remotes. Finally, consider having at least one of the lamps on a timer. It's more welcoming than a dark home and serves as a deterrent for burglars.

FINE DINING

In a majority of homes, the dining room and living room are adjacent to each other. It's essential that the design be consistent from room to room. This can be done through using related colors, drapery fabrics, or furniture genre. A beach-style sofa in the living room and a spare contemporary dining table and chairs really don't work. Carry a theme and be consistent throughout the rooms.

Many of us grew up with the idea of having a dining room set: a table with matching chairs. Today, however, you are no longer expected to abide by those often-boring guidelines. I prefer mixing things up. Anyone can go out and buy a matching set, but mixing one style of table with a different style of chairs creates a more dynamic setting, and in designing, the goal is to create a

Hopp Tips:

- Buy lampshades in unusual shapes. Soft sided fabric shades cast a warm glow and you can have them made in coordinating fabric to match your décor.

- In months when a fireplace isn't lit, stack logs with the ends facing out. Use as many as it takes to fill the opening. It creates a dramatic earthy effect. Make sure you check for spiders before you start!

- Reorganize your accessories by theme. They work better in multiples than single objects. Display them on a tray on a side table or in a bookcase. Not only do the groupings make a more dramatic statement, they keep a room from looking cluttered.

- Use chandelier shades on a dining room fixture. They add romance while reducing glare.

- Decorate a dining room wall with plates. Use different sizes, shapes and patterns. Lay out the design on the floor before hammering any nails. Or use the plates to create templates. You can drive the nails right through the templates and simply throw them away. It makes measuring much easier.

93

look more exciting than a dining room "set." Some of my favorite dining rooms are ones with mismatched chairs or host chairs that differ from the side chairs. Remember that our parents' rules don't have to apply. Whether the dining room chairs match or not, find ones that are comfortable. This may be an area where you should plan to invest a little more money because buying eight chairs can add up quickly. When creating the dining room, it is important to have chairs that you love to look at, and it's even better if you like to sit in them.

In a perfect blend of old and new, reed chairs work well with the dining table to establish an eclectic look. A church pew at the back of the room is dressed up with pillows to add color and softness. Chinese lanterns and a floral arrangement create a charming centerpiece.

In the dining room, the primary source of sound-absorbing material is the chairs, unless you have wall-to-wall carpeting. As in the living room, windows are where you employ additional layers for light control, sound absorption, and style. When you are planning draperies, the same rules apply here as in the living room. You need to consider both light control and what you want to accomplish with the draperies. Draperies always finish the look of the room and also make it feel more inviting than unadorned windows.

If you have a hard-surface flooring, a rug helps ground the room and define the dining area. It can also add color and create a formal or casual look, depending on the style you want. Again, there are so many options when it comes to rugs, you are sure to find something that does exactly what you want for the space. Make sure you buy rugs that are large enough. There is nothing worse than pulling out your chair and having it fall off the rug.

Don't forget something for the center of the dining table. Again, it's one of those things that complete your composition. A beautiful bowl filled with decorative ceramic balls or ones made from organic material like grass, wood, or seeds is attractive and easy to move. If you prefer candles, I strongly suggest staying away from the traditional two candlestick arrangements with tapers in them. Instead, use seven or eight candlesticks of varying heights. It's more exciting than what one would traditionally see, and people take notice when they see something unexpected. Or instead of candles, consider a floral arrangement on your table. Since replacing real flowers every few days can be expensive, consider artificial florals. The challenge is to find an arrangement that does not look obviously fake. You want people to have to touch it to discover whether it is real or not.

There are few things worse than dining in glaring light. Think of how a good restaurant dims the lights to make the experience special. Since most of us don't eat in our dining room every night, the experience we create when entertaining or dining should be special too. Again, dimmers are the solution. I like to use candles and turn the dimmer on so low that it appears the room is being lit solely by the candles. This creates an atmosphere that is not only intimate but also more relaxing.

The chandelier is often the focal point of the dining room. If it's not a wonderful fixture, then replace it. As I discussed in the section about the kitchen and the breakfast room, home builders generally don't put much of an investment in the light fixtures that come with the house. Changing the chandelier creates a dramatic difference in the overall feel of a dining room. Don't worry about matching the kitchen or breakfast room fixtures. This is one of those instances when the fixture stands on its own. Dress it up or down—however you

want—to suit the look for your dining room. If you have bare bulbs, use chandelier shades to soften the light. If a new fixture isn't in your budget, paint the existing one a suitable color. I have seen people use bronze, white, black, and red. Be creative. It's your house.

In place of a traditional dining table, an outdoor table base paired with a large glass top. The dramatic centerpiece is mercury glass candle holders from Ikea with extra tall tapers. Simple lampshades eliminate glare at the chandelier, while lamps on the buffet illuminate the art and floral arrangement.

CHAPTER 7
BATHING BEAUTIES

THE BATHROOM

"Even a small indulgence can mean a big change in the bathroom."
–Nate Berkus

As with the kitchen, the evolution of the bathroom during the last couple of decades has been astonishing. What was simply a white bath—basic sink, simple toilet, and tub—has now emerged as a world of color, finishes, and new features. Have you noticed lately the number of magazines that are solely devoted to bathrooms? What was a utilitarian necessity is now operating as a refuge. Today's newer bathrooms are larger and brighter, with more luxurious fixtures and materials that elevate the bath to a place to spend quality time in.

Congratulations to those who have one of those baths. I myself always wanted a bathroom large enough for a lounge chair. In the end, it probably would be a towel holder; still, I think it would be glamorous. For most of us, however, the glamour bath is in the future, and we have to make do with smaller spaces. The trick is how to create a blissful bath and still have money to buy new towels. Let's start talking about inexpensive makeovers that create a huge difference.

VANITY FLAIR

One of the most dramatic changes to a bath is replacing the vanity. This is easier than ever because premade vanities are more common, so you don't have to go custom to get a designer look. Premade vanities come in a variety of styles and materials that can fit décor from contemporary to traditional. Vanities are becoming more like furniture than just sink cabinets with convenient places for bathroom storage. Many come with small legs that you would find on a dresser, and some have knobs on the drawers that definitely get designer approval. With the Internet, you can find a number of sources, so you don't have to drive all over town to locate something you may like. Order them online, and have them delivered right to your home. Online catalogues such as Home Decorators Collection

have complete packages, including a stone top, sink, and faucets. I have seen designs at Home Depot and Lowes that would look perfect in homes ranging from Craftsman to French Country as well as contemporary.

Pre-made vanities provide a cost effective and stylish makeover for this bath. Bath towels are conveniently stored below the vanity in reed baskets. Flowers and accessories finish the space while keeping the room uncluttered.

A custom made mirror at the bathroom vanity is a nice decorating note. Lighting is provided by nickel scones that match the sink faucet and bath hardware. Countertop items are artfully displayed and ready to use.

MIRROR, MIRROR

Many bathrooms have a long frameless mirror over the vanity. Get rid of it! Those mirrors are the least expensive choice for bathrooms and are a contractor staple. If you prefer a large mirror over the vanity, consider using molding to create a framed look, or use tile around the mirror and incorporate it in the backsplash. It's a much better look than an unfinished mirror. If you can remove the mirror, replace it with a single framed mirror or one above each sink. When designing and staging homes, I always get mirrors made by my framer Willging. The advantage is that you can do a custom size and pick your own frame. If you prefer to buy off the shelf, Home Depot or Lowes is an option, and do not forget to check out flea markets and antique stores; there is nothing like an old mirror. Changing the mirror is one of the more dramatic and simple things you can do to transform your bathroom to a space that looks as great as the rest of the house.

TAKE YOUR MEDICINE (CABINET)

What happened to medicine cabinets in bathrooms? For that matter, with all the changes in bath design, why isn't there more storage? Today, builders seem to focus on creating huge clothes closets and taking away linen closets that used to be in most bathrooms from the past. Personally, I think a medicine cabinet is practical. The items you use daily are kept at eye level. Newer homes simply put in a large mirror and expect us to use the drawers. The neglected medicine cabinet is a simple fix. The selection is no longer a white box with a metal-framed mirror. Newer cabinets have oval doors or wood-trimmed doors, and some have mirrored interiors with electrical outlets, which are practically a must for electric toothbrushes. If you have plumbing or electrical obstacles, consider a cabinet that is not recessed. While it may project a bit, it is easy to hang, and if it does not present an obstacle to using the sink, it is well worth the compromise.

Often, a small cabinet, a set of shallow shelves, or an étagère that sits above your toilet's tank can provide extra storage your bathroom sorely needs. Oft-used items such as extra hand towels or rolls of toilet paper can be stored in these useful bathroom cabinets.

Medicine cabinets provide the best bathroom storage. Planned in advance the medicine cabinet can be framed in molding to blend seamlessly with the room's design. Recessed cabinets are preferable because they are less intrusive.

THE POWER OF PAINT

If time or money is an issue, you can borrow the idea discussed in the kitchen, and simply paint the cabinets. Never underestimate the power of paint. It can transform dated dark wood cabinets into bright stylish vanities that you would see in fine homes. Avoid bold colors as you will tire of them in a short time. It is best to stick with whites and paler colors such as sea glass or Aegean blue. As with any paint job, it's all in the prep work. Sand, sand, sand the existing finish! Especially on wood-grain cabinets. Paint will adhere better on a well-prepared surface, and no one wants to paint the same thing twice.

Semigloss paints are better for bathrooms than a flat or eggshell finish. The reason is that flat and eggshell paints are more likely to absorb moisture. In a room that receives more humidity than anywhere else, you will want a finish that can be easily wiped down.

Many clients I have worked with in the past used the default color—white—everywhere in the bathroom. As in the kitchen, find your style and express yourself. Paint is a dramatic change on your walls as much as it is on your cabinets. Remember that walls reflect color. Avoid green or yellow paints that make you look sickly or sallow. You want colors to lift you up and make you look good! Bathrooms that have a great deal of light can handle darker, more intense colors. Remember that dark colors absorb light, so if you want a bright bathroom, stick with lighter shades.

Save the drama for rooms like a powder room that you aren't using daily. I am all for drama—at least on the walls.

If you are uncertain about the paint or how it will look in the bathroom, buy a sample can or even several different colors. Most paint stores now offer sample paints that can be used to test colors. The sample container may only hold a cup or so of paint, but it's enough for you to decide whether you like it or not. Often what looks good at the paint store under a different set of bright lights will look much different in a bath that uses incandescent lighting. Look at the painted samples at different times of day to see how the color will look in different types of light.

Fresh paint and new cabinet knobs is the fastest bathroom makeover imaginable.

THE RIGHT LIGHT

The bathroom is the activity center for shaving, makeup, and washing. Proper lighting is crucial. The best type of lighting is a wall sconce on either side of the mirror. This is called cross illumination. This brings the light to eye level and illuminates both sides of the face. This is much better lighting for the bathroom than the strip of lights above the mirror or vanity. Strip lighting is only great at illuminating the ceiling and the top of your head. The worst lighting for a bathroom is a recessed can light. Recessed lights cast shadows on the face, especially if you lean in towards the mirror. You end up looking ghoulish with the lower part of your face in the dark.

Bathroom lighting fixtures are one of the easiest types to find. The large hardware stores have a vast selection. This is probably a good time to return to your style file. What type of fixture do you see in the rooms in your photos? Once you have narrowed that down, there still are many choices. Online searches are a smart way of seeing products. Lightinguniverse.com and lampsplus.com are sources that offer a huge assortment. Looking at the sites, you can narrow your selection by style, finish, number of lamps, and type of light-bulb. Even narrowing your search criteria, you will still have hundreds of choices.

An internet search will offer a multitude of options and ideas for a stylish bath. Look at these before you drive anywhere!

- Bedbathandbeyond.com
- Lightinguniverse.com
- Homedecorators.com
- Lowes.com
- Homedepot.com

Final touches on the counter—fragrance diffusers and soap dispensers keep the room fresh and tidy.

FINAL TOUCHES

Bathroom hardware is another important feature. Obviously, we want the hardware to match the plumbing fixtures. However, there aren't hard and fast rules. You may have a nickel faucet and find that bronze towel bars and toilet paper holders work better. Generally, if I use a finish different from the plumbing, I make sure that at least it matches the finish on light fixtures or door hardware.

Towel rings have never seemed practical to me. They only hold one towel that has to be bunched up to fit through the opening, so the towels never dry properly. Towel bars make much better sense. Decorative hooks are even better. They can be mounted by the shower for convenient access to your towel, and they allow for more ventilation to dry a towel that otherwise may take longer folded up on a towel bar.

At a client's house, they used dinner napkins instead of hand towels in the main powder room. Aside from thinking it was chic, I realized how practical and sanitary it was. Fresh napkins to dry your hands on are much more sanitary than hand towels that are used by many. Keep this in mind at your next party; your guests will thank you! There are wooden trays that you can use to keep the napkins organized, and if you want to go all out, you can find napkins with your monogram!

Apothecary jars filled with loofahs, bath salts and soaps fill an unused corner at the tub while framed botanical prints are a pretty focal point. Striped romans over woven grass shades are a perfect combination allowing light into the bath while providing softness at the window.

Bathrooms are the smallest rooms in the house, so it is important to keep them free of clutter. A hamper is practical in the bathroom; however, it is rarely attractive. Most bathrooms do not include room for one, so hampers are always in the way. My advice: Get them out of the bathroom. If you want a hamper in the bathroom, you may be able to find a spot for it under a vanity or in a deep drawer. Home improvement stores have kits to create a built-in hamper that can be pulled out for easy access. It is a simple project that will keep the room tidy. Still, the hamper should be emptied at least every other day so that damp towels can dry and not get mildew. No one likes that smell!

Honestly, when was the last time you changed that plastic liner? Decorative outer shower curtains are another item that can pull together your bathroom. Florals, stripes, colors, and novelty curtains are just some of the selections to upgrade the bath. Even if the tub already has an enclosure, a curtain is still a smart choice to hide an unattractive shower door or messy shower. I have used drapery panels meant for windows to hide a shower. The panels are much longer than shower curtains, and using two panels can create a more luxurious look. Drapery panels come in sizes ranging from 84 inches to 108 inches, so the curtain can extend from floor to ceiling. No matter what you choose, a little fabric goes far in pulling together a bath design.

Strangely enough, bathrooms are one of the better places in the house to hang art. There is usually space above a towel bar, toilet, or water closet walls if you have a separate one. When staging homes, we always looked for a focal point. Which wall demands the most attention? That's the wall that should have a piece of art. Take care to select something that can handle the amount of humidity; this isn't the room to hang valuable artwork. For example, wooden plaques work well, and framed pieces are a natural. The vanity counter is a good spot for decorative art as long as it doesn't interfere with the function or make the counters look cluttered. Stores such as Ross and Marshalls carry inexpensive pieces that are perfect in a bath.

Keep soaps, salts and sponges close at hand in glass apothecaries. Indulge yourself and use them!

Hopp Tips:

- I like antique mirrors for powder rooms. The scale of older mirrors works better in smaller spaces and the mottling of vintage glass hides wrinkles and fine lines.

- Make your bathroom feel like a spa. Get rid of clutter and buy luxurious oversize towels. Use scented candles or reed diffusers - smells are important as sites in a bathroom. Be sure to use the candles. They are not only for show!

- Have a frame shop make a mirror for you. There are thousands of profiles. You can get them fabricated in any size and they can be a lot less expensive than pre-made designs at retail stores.

- If the bathroom light is pitted, chipped, damaged or dated, buy a new fixture. There is nothing like a clean bright light to make a bathroom feel fresh.

- Find artwork that will hold up to the humidity in a bathroom. Most bathrooms have walls perfect for art, and this room should be as pretty as the rest of the house.

Other decorative, but functional, items are scented candles, fragrance diffusers and soaps. These are inexpensive little luxuries, look great on countertops, and provide a clean, fresh-smelling scent to the bathroom. At the bathtub, use glass canisters filled with loofahs and sponges, bath salts (you can make your own from recipes online), or decorative soaps. Soaps come in all shapes and scents, do not cost much, and are easily replaced. So indulge yourself and use them! Candles next to the tub are particularly nice because they add a touch of romance and relaxation to create a quiet atmosphere. All of these bathroom extras are perfect on tubs with big decks—those pesky corners are always a challenge!

Plants are a smart accessory in the bath. Live plants can thrive in humidity, and since most bathrooms have natural light, they are in a healthy environment. If you don't have a green thumb, consider artificial arrangements. As I mentioned in other sections, there are artificial greens that work well, such as topiaries or a selection of interesting branches arranged in a vase or container. Bathrooms get dusty quickly, so make sure you are on top of the cleaning. Everything needs maintenance to look good.

If you add up all the time spent in the bathroom during the course of our lives, it would be months! While women have more tasks to do in the bathroom than men, studies show that men tend to dawdle more than women. Simple luxuries, smart solutions, art, and accessories enhance the environment. As long as we are in there, we might as well enjoy our surroundings. Planned well, your bathroom can be as appealing as any other room in the house. And why not? We deserve it!

Make your bathroom feel like a spa. Find simple luxuries that enhance the environment. Enjoy your bathroom as much as any other room in the house.

CHAPTER 8
IN MY ROOM

THE MASTER BEDROOM

"The bed has become a place of luxury to me! I would not exchange it for all the thrones in the world."
–Napoleon

Like the kitchen and bathroom, the master bedroom has seen a dramatic shift in the last few decades. The rooms have become much larger, and that has created the opportunity for more than just sleeping. Amenities that were once thought of as luxuries have become standard. It is now common practice for the master bedroom to have a private bath. The master often has an office, a lounge chair to read to the kids before bed, and, of course, a TV where we zone out prior to going to sleep. Naturally, the choice of activities is yours. As a designer, my goal is to create a sanctuary that is a soothing, romantic refuge that you don't want to leave as it becomes another of your favorite rooms in the house.

GET AHEAD (BOARD)

The main focal point of the master bedroom is the bed. You may have a view, a fireplace, or a television, but the most important item in the room is the bed. It's usually the first thing you see upon entering the room, and it sets the tone for the space. Your bed becomes the item that other furniture in the room is based upon or around. When working with clients, the bed is the piece I choose first.

I am always surprised when I see a bedroom without a headboard. I tend to use the word *headboard* generically to mean anything above and beyond the frame, box spring, and mattress. It is probably one of the easiest items to find, and when shopped properly, it can be reasonably priced. My experience in home staging has helped me serve my clients even better. When staging, I had to be very mindful of our budget, both in terms of money and time. I started shopping the readily available stores so I could walk away with a design I liked. Pier 1 Imports quickly became a favorite because it has a wonderful selection of styles, and the pricing is unbelievable. Another resource I found is jcpenney.com. Its pricing for iron and upholstered headboards, two of my favorites, is very affordable.

With an endless list of style options, you can create just about any look with the right headboard. It can be anything: wrought iron, wood, fabric, or unique materials. I have seen designs where the headboard was a converted five-panel door and one that was the top to a baby grand piano. For a particularly adventurous client, I created a headboard from a Balinese handrail. It suited the eclectic interior and made the bed stand out as one of a kind. I have even seen designs painted directly on the wall behind the bed that served as the headboard—a brilliant idea for the spatially challenged. Having a headboard isn't so much that the bed needs one; it's the idea that it completes the bed. A couple of pillows leaning against the wall isn't the focal point we want to create and doesn't give a very luxurious "welcome."

The headboard is the most important item in creating a focal point in the bedroom. Mix wood and paint finishes and avoid buying boring bedroom sets. Make the space uniquely yours.

In recent years, the interior designer's favorite—the upholstered headboard—has become available almost everywhere. One of the things I like about it is that you can select a number of different styles. From a simple square shape to a more exotic design with a lot of curves, the choice is yours, and when you add in the number of fabric options, the world is your oyster. The upholstery, like iron, becomes a neutral in the room, which means you aren't stuck with matching a wood tone to the other items in the room, such as a nightstand, an armoire, or a chest of drawers. The reason designers like it is that it doesn't match all the furniture.

Back in the days of Lucy and Ricky, the matching bedroom set was the thing to have. (So were twin beds, and you do not see those in master bedrooms anymore either). The problem with a bedroom set is that it is boring. You are designing your personal space, and that should be uniquely yours. Sets do not allow for much creativity. A matching bedroom set looks like it has been purchased all at once, probably because it has been. You want your bedroom to reflect your personal

taste and show that you live there, not as if you moved into a showroom! One thing done well in hotel design is that items are coordinated to work well together even when they don't match. In your bedroom, furniture does not have to match to work together. The next time you go through your design file, look at what others do. I think you will be pleasantly surprised.

Old window frames are a clever and affordable way to frame art or, in this case, wallpaper. Whimsical flea market lamps add character, while shabby chic linens from Target against an upholstered headboard cap off this bedrooms vintage appeal.

In front of a window, an iron headboard allows light through while providing a backdrop for handsome blue and white linens. My mother's fur coat was repurposed as a pillow that gives the appearance of a luxurious extravagance. Masculine dark lampshades add to the room's elegant simplicity.

ONE NIGHT STANDS

If your bed wall is large enough to accommodate jumbo-sized side tables, I say go for it. I generally select tables 30 inches wide or more. Once a lamp, clock, and phone are placed on it, there is little room for a book, a glass of water, or whatever else you might want close at hand. We spend one-third of our lives in bed (granted it's mostly sleeping), so have the things around you that you want nearby. Make it convenient so you can stay in bed longer, and who doesn't love that?

Like the headboard, the night tables can be anything. Mixing finishes, styles, and materials keeps a room interesting, so if there is a lot of wood in the room, consider something different for the nightstand. If you bought a matching set, think about splitting it up and using the nightstands in another room. With wood, a painted finish is a great alternative to a traditional stain. You can paint an unusual color that is a contrast for the rest of the room, or even use a color that becomes a neutral in the room. For a romantic look, use a skirted table with a beautiful tablecloth on top. Finish off the look with a glass top as it makes the table more serviceable. One of my favorite alternatives to a traditional nightstand is an antique table. There is nothing quite like the patina of an old piece to add charm and character to a bedroom.

The patina of the large Asian altar table is a perfect mix with the contemporary table lamp. Useful drawers keep things close at hand, and the arrangement of artificial lilies and softness and romance to the room.

THE FLIP OF A SWITCH

What would our bedroom sanctuary be without proper lighting? Bedside lighting can not only serve the task of reading in bed, but lamps with shades also help light up the room with a soft glow. Elaborate or simple, made of crystal, metal, or even converted old tea canisters, the table lamp is a style workhorse adding to the design scheme. Shop your style; if you have a contemporary look, sleek, minimalist lamps help define it. If you tend toward traditional, narrow down your preferences. Do you like metal? Crystal? Wood? It's out there; now it's up to you to find it. I usually start with Pottery Barn. Their styles change continually, and they sell shades separately from bases, so you can put together something that is just right for the look you want. If space is limited, use a swing-arm lamp mounted on either side of the headboard. The advantage of swing-arm lamps is that they can be positioned right where you need the light for reading. Styles range from rustic to modern or gilded brass.

For some reason, people tend to use smaller lamps for bedside tables. I think this is the influence of the days when the tables were small. The biggest problem is that they tend to be short, which makes them the wrong scale for most master bedrooms. They take up the same amount of space on the side table, so don't be afraid to go for lamps with more height and a bigger shade. Look at the same-size lamp that you would use in the living room or family room. The taller styles are better with

the scale of a bed, and you want light to be above you, not below. Don't forget shades! They have a huge impact on both the style and quantity of light. Avoid opaque shades in the bedroom if they are to be used for reading. This type of shade only casts light up and down. You will be leaning over to get enough light to read.

One final note about lamps at the bedside: Use a line switch on the cord. They are easier to reach, and they have a high/low switch to adjust the light for reading or other activities. It's a small fix, and well worth the effort.

Full size table lamps at the bedside are a better scale in most bedrooms. Use a line switch on the cord—they are easier to reach.

115

Take a different approach when installing general lighting in the master bedroom from what you would with other spaces. The light is usually only for passing through or for cleaning. If you have recessed lighting, remember to put the lights on a dimmer switch. If you have a center fixture in the ceiling, look for one that continues your overall theme. The traditional approach is to have a close-to-the-ceiling fixture. However, if you have space, a pendant fixture is as stylish as it is functional. Just make sure it doesn't hang so low that you will hit your head. Finally, if you must have a ceiling fan, be certain that the light and fan are on separate switches. Newer models have remotes, which is a feature that you will surely appreciate when you're just too tired—or too comfy—to get out of bed.

Shop at discount stores like Marshalls, Ross and Homegoods for linens. The other sites listed are great resources for bedroom furniture, lighting and accessories. You will be surprised with how many styles and designs are available.

- Pineconehill.com
- Thecompanystore.com
- Potterybarn.com
- Urbanoutfitters.com
- Garnethill.com
- Ballarddesigns.com
- Westelm.com

HIDE AND SEEK

I hate seeing a big television in the master bedroom; it sucks the romance right out of the room. I admit though that I do enjoy watching TV from bed. So what's an HGTV lover to do? The designer trick that has gone main-stream is hiding the television in an armoire. These days, armoires are easy to find and come from most manufacturers. Now that the popularity and affordability of flat-screen TVs has grown, many people have moved toward mounting them on the wall. While this is less obtrusive than the oversized boob tubes of days gone by, it's still not quite as nice as having the TV out of sight.

An armoire or tall cabinet is an ideal solution when you need a hiding spot for your TV. Just open the doors when you want to veg out with the tube on and voila! Many armoires now come with recessed doors to minimize the amount of space taken up by this versatile piece of furniture. What's even better is that armoires come with some extra benefits. They add vertical balance and scale to the room since most pieces of furniture in the bedroom are horizontal—the headboard, table surfaces, mattress, and so forth. The armoire changes this while providing visual interest. Additionally, armoires offer more storage, and that's something that just about everybody needs.

If your television is mounted on the wall and you want it to stay there, invest in cord covers to hide the wires. You can paint the covers to match the color of your wall for a neat, seamless effect. If there are additional components to your television, such as a cable box or DVD player, avoid placing them on the dresser. Simply put, it never looks good. Keep these out of sight, yet still accessible, by investing in an armoire with a mesh or glass door that will still allow the remote control's signal to reach.

The armoire is an important piece when setting the style in the room. If you tend toward antiques, vintage clothes cabinets and traditional armoires are perfect. I've taken older pieces and painted them to create a distressed look, and they became a neutral that blends well with the other furniture. IKEA and Crate and Barrel have cabinets with clean, simple lines that work better in modern environments. Or there are a number of Asian cabinets that are a stylish choice for either. Remember, like the nightstands, the armoire or cabinet doesn't have to match the other furniture. An attractive coordinating piece goes far in bedroom style.

Aside from armoires, bookcases are perfect for storage in bedrooms. While it all depends on the room's layout, bookcases add to the coziness of the space while providing important storage. Baskets or boxes mixed with family photos and books create a comfortable atmosphere you may never want to leave.

Tall cabinets are important for scale in a bedroom and they serve double duty by hiding the television. The black finish blends well with the vintage night tables. White lamps and linens keep the room bright against the periwinkle paint color.

LOUNGING AROUND

As master bedrooms have increased in size, the opportunity for additional seating has come along. If you want to escape the hustle and bustle of everyday life and unwind in a peaceful space, a comfortable lounge chair in the master bedroom is a must. A good lounge chair is one that provides support while allowing you to get comfortable. What is comfortable to you will largely depend on your personal needs. Do you prefer a chair that you can just sink into and relax, or does your back need a little more support? Go for a test-drive, sit in all the chairs that appeal to you, see which you like best, and which will meet your personal needs. Also, consider the materials of which a chair is made. A wood-framed chair might not be the best option for comfort even if it looks nice. More important, would you use it if you owned it? Do not buy a chair just for looks alone; take the time to find one that feels as good as it looks. Once you have found the perfect chair, complete your new refuge with the addition of a good reading lamp, a side table, and a pile of books!

A painted farmhouse style headboard creates a strong focal point. Black becomes a neutral in this room so other woods can be mixed without clashing. Large skirted tables add softness and much needed scale. A reed lounge chair in the corner is a comfortable refuge.

UNDER THE COVERS

Good linens are not a luxury; they are a necessity. This is one area in which I love to educate my clients. I am a big fan of 100% cotton sheets. While there are other options, pure cotton sheets let the body breathe at night and are generally softer and lighter than cotton-polyester blends. When splurging on good sheets, the most important factor to consider is thread count. Thread count simply refers to the number of threads in a single square inch of fabric. Generally, the higher the thread count, the softer the sheet. Other elements come into play when determining the softness of a fabric, such as the size of the thread. Thinner threads allow for a greater number of threads to fit into one square inch. Finer threads create softer and smoother sheets, which is what makes high-thread-count sheets so desirable. Next time you are at a store, feel the difference between 200-count and 400-count sheets, and you'll see what I mean. If you can, do not go below a 400 thread count. Not only do higher counts feel better, they last longer through frequent laundering.

You will also want to consider the knit of the sheets—percale, jersey, flannel or sateen. Percale is very closely woven and has a silky feel. It is considered to be one of the finest available. Jersey knit is very loose and elastic. Flannel, which is a wintertime favorite, is twill woven in such a way that leaves a napped finish. This is what creates that little layer of fluff that's so cozy on a cold night. Sateen is a very soft lustrous weave that is accomplished by using a greater amount of yarn surface on the face of the cloth.

Hopp Tips:

- Choose the headboard before you select anything else in the room. The bed is the focal point, so it should make an impact. Headboards are a smart way to add a different finish such as iron, paint or upholstery.

- Do not buy bedroom sets. Select items that coordinate well together. Push the envelope of your creativity. Design a personal space that is uniquely yours.

- Soften windows with drapery. Drapery is one of the best ways to finish windows while adding romance in the bedroom. Add black out lining if you like to keep your room dark.

- New bedding is the fastest way to make a bedroom feel fresh again. Many stores have gorgeous, sophisticated patterns that won't break the bank. Start at the sales rack first!

- Use the largest night table that will fit comfortably in the room. A larger scale is better proportion with beds, and it's convenient to have a generous surface for essentials. If you can find a piece that has drawers, you will appreciate the storage.

While staging, I bought most of the bedding from stores like Marshalls, Ross, or even Tuesday Morning. These stores carry high-end linens at deeply discounted prices where I've found luxurious sheets from expensive manufacturers on many shopping trips. Like anything, it's the luck of the draw and takes a little digging. Still, it is worth the effort because the savings are tremendous, and the selection is often quite good.

The best way to make a bed is to use a fitted sheet, a top sheet, a blanket, and then a blanket cover, which some people might call a bedspread. In cooler climates, it is smart to use a duvet folded at the bottom of the bed that can be pulled up at night for warmth. If you live in a warmer climate, you may not need a duvet. Instead, toss a light throw or blanket across the bottom of the bed to add color. For example, if you have a white blanket cover, an Oxford blue throw adds style; where a white bedspread might be kind of dull, the touch of color makes an eye-catching difference.

Changing beddings is pretty easy and inexpensive, and it can completely transform a bed. For staging a house, it is at the top of the list. A new bedspread and/or a duvet and new pillow shams are a dramatic difference. Consider different beddings for different seasons or looks, depending on what you want to do. You might have a green blanket cover with ivory sheets or white and chocolate. When the sheets need laundering, switch the set with another and keep things interesting.

COME TO MY WINDOW

Because the most important function of the master bedroom is creating a haven where you can achieve a night of restful sleep, it is important to understand how you sleep. For example, does having any light in the room bother you, or do you prefer being awakened by the morning sun? Do you enjoy an afternoon nap and a dark room? The type of window coverings you select will depend on the amount of light you want in your room throughout the day. You should also consider preventing heat loss or heat gain and preventing people from seeing inside if these are concerns you have.

Woven wood roman style shades provide light control and add contrast in this light filled bedroom. Patterned wall paper adds texture, and the upholstered headboard is a fun and colorful addition.

If you like a dark room, the best window treatment is a blackout drapery. This is most commonly found in hotel rooms. A blackout fabric is a dense fabric used as a lining that keeps out most light. Although many people like wood blinds or woven wood shades for controlling light, the problem is there is still light leakage that can drive you crazy when all you want is the comfort of darkness to help you rest. If you are one of those people, then a blackout drapery is the best way to address the problem.

If having a dark room isn't that important to you, I suggest woven wood shades. Woven woods are made of a woven grass, bamboo, or a very thin wood. I think they are spectacular because they block out the bulk of the harsh sunlight, and you can still see out of them. They have an organic look that works well in traditional settings as well as in contemporary. Bear in mind that at night when your light is on, people can see in. If that is a concern, you can complement the woven woods with a Roman shade or drapery that will allow for complete privacy when it is drawn.

Aside from being functional, window treatments finish a room. They are sort of the cherry on top of the icing on the cake. There are a multitude of options to choose from, which can make it overwhelming when deciding on the look and feel you want to create. You may opt for an uncomplicated, straightforward design in a contemporary home, or a more elaborate style in traditional settings. Fabric always adds softness and

Drapery is one of those elements that make a bedroom welcoming. The softness of the fabric absorbs sound, and are the finishing touch for windows. If light control is an issue, use black out lining to keep the room dark.

This handsome bedroom shows how to pull off a monochromatic color scheme by varying patterns. Linens create the direction for this room and the black and white theme gets carried throughout the art and accessories. The headboard is an affordable find from a hotel surplus store using a simple black tablecloth to recover the upholstered portion. Lamps and shades, bought separately and combined add a playful element to the space.

gives a romantic appearance. If you choose to use wood blinds, consider decorative side hangings that flank the window opening. Using decorative side panels will not change the amount of light coming into a room. They will, however, give a more polished look and create a softness that is especially nice in a bedroom.

Do your homework, and look online for premade draperies. Premade draperies come in a range of sizes that will accommodate most windows, so finding something to suit your needs shouldn't be difficult. Often, it is considerably less expensive than going the route of custom-made. If you can save money while accomplishing your design, why pay the big bucks? It will give your budget a boost, and you can spend the savings somewhere else. After all, staying on budget is bliss!

COLOR ME BEAUTIFUL

The impact of color is important in the bedroom because you want to choose a color that is calming and relaxing. You may choose to use wallpaper or faux finishes; however, the master bedroom isn't a place to experiment with outrageous colors. Avoid bright or hot colors, which are more energizing than soothing. This isn't the place for dramatic reds and exciting oranges. The colors you select need to relax and prepare you for sleep and also gently greet you when you awake.

When choosing colors for fabrics, refer to your design file. Remember, this is the place where you keep pictures you have cut from magazines or pictures from your cell phone of items that you like. Creating bliss takes time and careful thought and consideration; fully armed with your reference materials, your style will come together as you notice the similarities throughout your pictures.

I often look at hotels for inspiration. Hotels have really stepped up their designs in recent years and are a useful source of ideas. Most typical hotel rooms will have four fabrics: the drapery, bedspread, bed skirt, and upholstery. Rarely are the fabrics the same. They don't have the same texture or pattern, and might not even be the same color, but they all work well together. The reason the fabrics aren't the same is that many items wear and fade at different rates. Having coordinating fabrics allows wear and tear to be less noticeable because one item's fabric can't be compared directly to another item in the room. There may be a mix of florals and stripes, but they work well together. Apply this idea to your bedroom. If you are working with fabrics in the same color scheme, such as blue and white, you can mix paisley and a striped damask, two completely different patterns, to create a cohesive look that is uniquely your own. Have fun mixing colors too! As many people who color their hair know, you don't have to match the carpet to the drapes to have it all work together.

FLOOR IT

My own preference and what I generally select when designing a master bedroom for a client is wall-to-wall carpeting. No one likes to get out of bed in the morning and step on a cold floor. The texture of a sumptuous carpet underfoot is much more pleasing, plus a carpet offers other benefits to the master bedroom. Not only does a carpet add texture, it also introduces more color and is an effective way to absorb sounds, so they won't reverberate in an irritating way.

If you have certain allergies or unruly pets, solid surface flooring may be a better choice. Hardwood will look lovely and is warmer, both visually and to the touch, than alternatives such as stone or tile. Since wood is a neutral, it works with any style in any setting. To pull the room together, top off your hardwood floor with a fabulous rug or two.

This striking master bedroom is all about the bed. Embroidered sheer panels transform this iron four poster bed into a romantic retreat. The white bedding is a calming contrast to the dramatic brown linen drapery from Marshalls. The brown and white West Elm geometric rug keeps this room casual. Woven spaghetti screen panels from Pier 1 provide a simple, effective, and affordable solution for window treatments and add to the allure of this peaceful sanctuary.

PART THREE
STUFF

KEEP YOUR EYE ON THE PRIZE

Editing clutter often unearths your home's most gorgeous features. A few years back, I staged a home that had a large fireplace in the living room. It wasn't until the seller removed her clutter that we discovered the beautiful and ornately carved mantel that was hiding underneath the sloppily draped fabric and dusty artificial flower arrangements. The dramatic fireplace ended up being a strong selling point for the home.

CHAPTER 9
ORGANIZING IT

"A house is just a place to keep your stuff while you go out and get more stuff."
–George Carlin

I probably should be the last one giving advice on organization. You should see my office! Nonetheless, clutter can take over your life. It may not look like clutter to you; it's just your stuff. Trust me, to everyone else its clutter! It can have a negative impact by making you feel that you have thousands of things to do. Why not tackle them, one at a time; put your mind at ease and live in the dream home you want to create.

Clutter isn't necessarily messy or spread about. Are there magazines stacked up here and there? Dog toys stashed in the corner? Baskets filled with random junk? That's all clutter. Most of the clutter around your home will probably be stuff that you think of as part of your everyday life. Clutter accumulates out of negligence. In my experience, the stuff that has built up out of neglect often holds no value—sentimental or otherwise—and is usually trash. It seems its sole purpose is to collect dust on your surfaces and make your house look messy.

It may seem overwhelming at first, and you may hear yourself asking, "Where do I begin?" If you think you are going to get the entire house done in one day, you are kidding yourself. Instead of setting yourself up for disappointment, create a win by setting reasonable goals. Start with the room you spend the most time in and tackle the floor first. Pick up all that stuff and take it out of the room. Create a space to sort it later so you don't lose your momentum. The sense of accomplishment will be well worth the effort.

Once the floors are clear, work your way up. Tabletops should have no more than three items on them. The "three object" rule comes in pretty handy throughout the entire editing and decorating process. Anything more than three either looks like a collection or looks like clutter. It detracts from the beauty of the architecture and furniture and often creates a sense of disorder in a room. It's surprising how great your tabletops look with less stuff on them.

Choose only the items that have the most meaning for you and that are most suitable to your personal style.

133

Useful baskets provide additional storage and are a great way to stay organized.

It is easy to get overwhelmed by electronic gadgets. Store appliances out of sight. You might be shocked at how huge your countertops appear once they are purged of clutter.

Once you can see your tabletops again, you will know it is time to tackle the mantels and shelves. A mantel is an important focal point in any room and is an important feature in your home. To start, remove everything from your mantel or shelves. Then choose a look suitable to your style. Candlesticks, plants, or art pieces are the usual choices. Again, there should not be more than three items. This rule can be broken if you are doing a series of plants or ceramics; however, in this case, less really is more.

In the kitchen, you might be shocked at how huge your countertops appear once they are purged of clutter. One trick that most designers employ is storing all small appliances out of site. It's easy to get overtaken by electronic gadgets. Keep only what you use daily. Remove all the other stuff that takes up counter space: knife sets, cutting boards, cookbooks; if you have canisters, make sure they are filled, clean, and stylish.

When I was helping a friend "de-clutter," we found cans and boxes of food that expired more than 15 years ago. I will bet that half the items in your pantry are expired. So why are you keeping them? Would you ever eat them? Somehow having stuff around makes us feel better, but if it cannot be used, why waste valuable real estate in your home? It is very freeing to purge—unfortunately, too many people are afraid to do it.

Whether your bathroom has plenty of storage space or not, organizing is the first step to keeping it from looking cluttered. Throw out any old products you don't use, fold towels neatly, and use a wicker or plastic baskets to group small items such as first aid supplies or nail care kits together. Stack any magazines or newspapers in a magazine rack, and store extra rolls of toilet paper in a holder next to the toilet or in the sink vanity.

Hopp Tips:

- Take everything cluttering a room – candle sticks, vases, photos and put them on the kitchen counter. Then re-select items in new arrangements. Save half and switch it up later in the year.

- Buy a bottle of wine and invite a friend over to sort through the kitchen drawers and cabinets. It's much more fun than doing it alone. Then return the favor at their place.

- Give away anything you have not worn or used for 12 months. It's the best way to find room in your closets.

- Collect all your magazines and tear out only the articles that you are going to read or use. Toss the rest into the recycling bin.

- Cut the clutter by using the 3 item rule. No more than 3 items on any tabletop.

When was the last time you cleaned your closet? I mean, really sorted through it? Pretend you're moving, and you would have to pay to move the stuff. That should get you motivated. With clothes, use the one-year rule. If you haven't touched it in a year, get rid of it. How likely is it that you are going to miss it? And really, if you lose that extra pound or two, are you going to want to wear something that is several seasons old?

In a laundry room, keep counters clear for folding, and store extras out of sight.

Once you've emptied all the clutter from a room, create the time to sort it out. We have different kinds of clutter in our lives. There's the sentimental stuff, like the bronze cast of our first pair of baby shoes, or grandma's hand-crocheted blankets that are too small for anything useful. Put them in Ziploc bags or a box and store them out of the way. I know some things we can never throw out; make sure that you keep only what you will use.

For weekday sorting, pick smaller, more manageable areas to commit to: the piles of paper in the office, the shelves in the living room, and so forth. Save the big projects for the weekend or for days when you can get support from family or friends. Assign each person to a problem area, such as closets or even their own bedrooms. Getting support will make the workload lighter and maybe even more fun. Make a game out of it: Who can get rid of the most stuff? Who has the biggest piece of junk? Even cleaning out your house can be fun if you make it fun.

Use the 1 year rule. If you haven't touched it in a year, get rid of it. You won't miss it.

Fold towels neatly, and organize by color. Give away any extras that don't work in your decorating scheme.

Hopp Tips:

- Sort all incoming mail over a garbage can or recycling bin.

- Purge the pantry. Organize items by everyday use, occasional use or items to be donated to a food bank. Trash items that are beyond their expiration date.

- Buy beautiful fabric covered boxes in different shapes and sizes for organization. Use color to differentiate categories in your closet.

- Accessorize and organize your bookshelves. Take covers off hardback books and group them by color. Stand some vertically, some horizontally to add interest. Mix in photos or collectible items to finish the arrangement.

- Transform the bath by folding towels neatly; use plastic or wicker baskets to sort like things together; keep extra toilet paper in a holder next to the toilet or vanity.

TIME FRAME

Anything not used for 12 months is as good as garbage. Don't sit around creating reasons to keep these things when they are not serving you. We frequently buy things expecting to use them, then a year goes by, and they're still sitting unopened, taking up space in our homes. Kitchen junk ranks pretty high on this list. I know you thought you were going to use that bread machine, the bag sealer, the clever little gadget that came with a guarantee to make your life easier, but if you haven't used any of those items in a year, it is highly unlikely that you need them, or that you'll ever even use them.

On one of my de-cluttering kicks, I found myself collecting stacks of magazines scattered around the house. When I finally put them all together to sort through, I discovered that I had about 200 magazines, some of which dated back three years! Of course, I had great reasons for wanting to keep them all: "Well, this one has that great article on art deco furniture, and that

Boxes and bins for organizing can be found at discounters such as Homegoods. For plastic closet organizers, proper hangers and almost anything you could need, let your fingers do the walking online.

- Realsimple.com
- Organize.com
- Containerstore.com
- Homedepot.com
- Lowes.com

one has the guide for incorporating floral drapes into a masculine setting." Then I came to my senses: Why am I hording 200 magazines when I only want a page or two out of each one? I decided to take the few pages I wanted, file them in a binder, and toss the rest. The end result was a house-load of magazines whittled down to a 1-inch binder that has actually become useful. Really, who is going to go tearing through 200 magazines to find an article on antique lighting fixtures? Think about how much time and energy it costs to keep your clutter.

As you move from room to room on your de-cluttering mission, you may begin to wonder if the clutter will ever end. You may be scratching your head attempting to figure out how you ended up with so much stuff. You might even protest clearing clutter altogether! Don't let the avalanche of stuff stop you. Clutter has the amazing ability to make a room look smaller than it is. It makes your home's storage appear to be inadequate. It can even take an ordinary room and transform it into a dark, cramped, and unwelcoming space. Editing all of this unnecessary clutter from your home actually adds space to your home; it lets the rooms breathe and will make any space seem lighter and more inviting. De-cluttering is the best way to add square footage to your home without hiring a contractor.

CHAPTER 10
WHOSE STUFF
IS IT ANYWAY?

"The more you have, the more you are occupied. The less you have, the more you are free."
–Mother Teresa

Do you have the kind of friends and family members who like to leave a memento for you to remember each visit by? I know I do, and the stuff accumulates fast: a towel here, casserole dish there, random pairs of sunglasses, and leftover paperbacks. Unless you are a professional storage facility, there is no need for you to store someone else's clutter. Your house should not contain anything that does not belong to you.

If it's something you borrowed, now is the time to give it back. If you're embarrassed about how long you've had it and don't want to give it back, then get rid of it, and hope for the best. If your kids have left the nest and now live on their own, it's time for them to come by and pick up their stuff. If you've ended a relationship and you're storing your ex's belongings, now is the perfect time to let his or her stuff (and that old relationship) go.

We make up stories about why we should hold on to these random things, but the truth is this: If it's not important enough for the owner to come get it, then why are you bothering to keep it? What is important is that you have a clutter-free house.

TRASH IT!

Nobody likes to hear this, but a lot of stuff we hold on to is plain old garbage. Remember what you are doing here: eliminating clutter. Whether you want to pack garbage, store it, unpack it, place it in your new home, or just throw it out is entirely up to you, but I know which I'd prefer.

While sorting through everything you've collected from each room, keep trash bags on hand, and make sure there is room in the trash bins. We're not talking about ditching a knickknack here or a stack of papers there; we're talking about getting rid of anything that is not serving you or enhancing the appearance of your house. This includes accessories that no longer go with your motif, and even furniture that's lost its appeal. If it's not helping your house, it's hindering it.

Hopp Tips:

- Envision your house as you want it to look – free of clutter. Then make a commitment to change. Stuff doesn't just affect you, it affects everyone that lives or visits your home.

- Share your vision with your partner, spouse or children. No one is a mind reader and they may have a completely different idea for a given space.

- Enlist help in creating your vision. Getting rid of stuff can be emotional. It's important to share your feelings and have a cheerleader on your side to motivate your progress.

- Do not keep stuff that you might need one day. Don't let those items represent your future. Create room for dreams to come true.

- Think about how much clutter costs you and your home by decreasing the amount of useable space you have. You don't need a bigger house, you need less stuff.

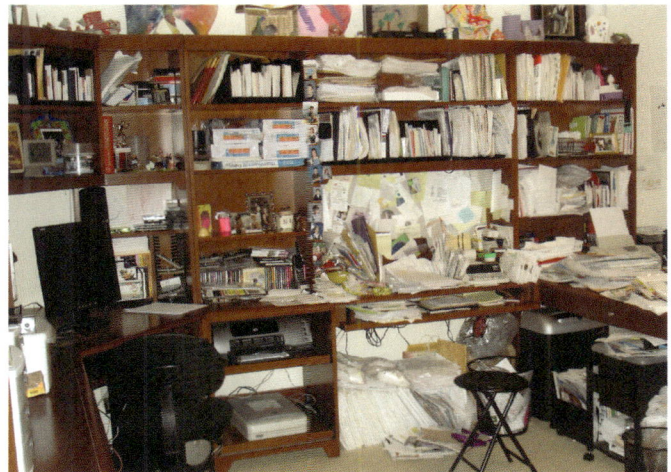

Clutter accumulates out of neglect.

DON'T FORGET

We've become so accustomed to living with certain things that they no longer register on our radar as clutter or as being simply out of place. The following list highlights some commonly overlooked items:

- Toys, stuffed animals, and playthings

- Sickly or dying plants

- Floral arrangements more than two years old

- Exercise equipment (unless you have a home gym)

- Pet paraphernalia such as cages, feeding dishes, litter boxes, and toys

- Cleaning supplies including mops, sponges, laundry baskets, and rags

- Personal grooming products such as brushes, perfumes, and makeup

- Medicine, vitamins, and dietary supplements

- Medical equipment

BIG PICTURE

Just clearing the clutter out of your house once won't solve the problem. Where else has stuff accumulated in your life? Can you park your car in the garage, or is it filled with things you "need"? Are you keeping the old TV because it cost a lot when you bought it? Do you even know where your VCR is? For that matter, when was the last time you watched a video as opposed to a DVD? How about the second refrigerator if you have one? Do you know what's in it? Was there a great sale on a side of beef that seemed like a good idea at the time? After a couple of trips to the second refrigerator or freezer, it often goes unused. There are many examples of things that have accumulated and just as many reasons for keeping them.

Garage sales: Your stuff gets a new life in someone else's home.

I recently liquidated some furniture and accessories I have been dragging around on the last several moves. I am guilty of the same thing as everyone else: a report I wrote in grade school, a Mickey Mouse watch I never looked at, dishes I was going to give to my niece, and a lamp that meant a lot to me—yet it was packed away in a box; I kept thinking I would use it in the next house. Old picture frames were supposed to be transformed into a collection of mirrors, and yet there they sat. Why was I keeping promotional items from movies or events when they only took up space?

Setting the stage for the sale made me aware of my attachment to things. Yet I made a commitment to rid myself of the things I really didn't need. As the sale progressed, it got easier, although when I sold something that had some emotion attached, it was like getting rid of a part of me. What was interesting to note was the thrill some buyers got in getting my "stuff." I realized that the joy these things had brought me was gone. (Otherwise I would have had them closer to me than a tattered box in storage). However, the joy that these things brought the buyer was noticeable. Sure, they sold for a fraction of the price of the original purchase, but they also were getting a new life in someone else's home, and in that way, the joy was passed along. The result in my life was less baggage—literally and figuratively. If I had done this sooner, I could have saved a bundle by not moving the "stuff" from location to location.

Living clutter free isn't a project you do once, and poof, you're done! It is an ongoing experience in which we ask ourselves, do I need this? Do I already have one of these? More important, will I use this? I recently read a book suggesting that for every new thing you bring into your home, you must remove one. Imagine how that would affect your decision making! Whatever method you choose, the goal is keeping yourself in check. Will it be used for decorating, or will I wear it? If you answer honestly, you will know what to do. It's time we stop fooling ourselves. In the end, you will discover living clutter free can be bliss!

Hopp Tips:

- Create time to clear clutter. It's an investment in yourself that will pay off with dividends.

- Do not offer to store items for someone else. Their clutter becomes your burden.

- Start with one room, clear everything out and only put in what supports the vision you have in mind. Enjoy having a space that makes you happy.

- Be honest, how much value does an item have if you never use or see it?

- Trash it or give it away. Make a time commitment to get rid of stuff and stick to it, and experience your home like you never have before.

CLOSING

BLISS!

I love coming home at the end of the day. My house is a refuge, a sanctuary, and it always makes me happy. Isn't that something we all want and crave? While I am not aware of it, subconsciously, the things I have in my house have energy, and I only keep ones that have positive energy. I think that is one thing that brings me happiness. I love the things I have collected, and they mean something. They are items that I have chosen through the years to put together my space.

If you're reading this book, it's clear you are interested in creating a home that reflects your style, vision, and experiences. Interior design is something we learn through time. Remember enlightened choice? It's the accumulated wisdom we have gained in order to make the right decisions confidently as we design our home. Enlightened choice is an ongoing process: Something we choose when we are 25 more than likely is not something we choose when we are 45.

There are many reasons our choices change through the years. It could be current fashion, a lack of funds, or even a lack of time to shop. As we learn and grow, we know more, and that affects our decision making. There is a knowledge gleaned from making mistakes (one of my least favorite ways of learning!). All of this factors into our decision making.

Our houses—our homes—are a reflection of who we are. The goal in interior design is identifying what pleases us most to create an environment we love. The result is the bliss that comes from a job well done and a place that always makes us happy!

ACKNOWLEDGMENTS

Thank you to all my clients because you have taught me the most about design. The opportunity to work with you to create spaces that you love has been the most cherished part of my work. From you, I've gained firsthand experience with everything from budgets to clutter, from designing around kids and pets to designing for romance and relaxation. Whether it was a minor renovation or a major construction project, working together to design your homes has been the greatest education I can imagine. You are the reason I am an interior designer, and you are the reason I still love my work!

Good photographers work magic in shooting a room. Thank you to Cristopher Lapp Still and Moving Images LLC; Joan Allen Photo; Alex Vasilescu Photography; Tria Giovan Photo; Tom Baker Photography. Thank you for making my work look great.

Particular thanks to my friends and colleagues for supporting me on this writing adventure: Liz Granite for researching and inspiring me, Julie Leaf for being the best cheerleader I've ever had, Allister Fong for managing all the madness of staging homes, and David Connella for his keen editorial revisions and support during the writing of this book.

Thank you to Mark Weaver for teaching me so much about design when I was new in the business and Randall Whitehead whose lighting expertise changed how I view a room.

Finally, a special note to Mom, who put up with a kid who moved furniture around endlessly. It is because of your love of decorating that I first became interested in interior design.

CPSIA information can be obtained
at www.ICGtesting.com
Printed in the USA
LVIW021513150113

315827LV00011B